edexcel

CW01640762

Edexcel Mathematics A Linear Access Practice Book

Series Director: Keith Pledger
Series Editor: Graham Cumming

Authors:
Julie Bolter
Gareth Cole
Gill Dyer
Michael Flowers
Karen Hughes
Peter Jolly
Joan Knott
Jean Linsky
Graham Newman
Rob Pepper
Joe Petran
Keith Pledger
Rob Summerson
Kevin Tanner
Brian Western

ALWAYS LEARNING

PEARSON

About this book

Welcome to the Access Practice Book for Edexcel!

The more you practise Maths, the better you will get. This book gives you lots of extra questions so that you can really get to grips with the Maths you will need in your GCSE exam. There are questions here for every chapter in your GCSE Maths Foundation Student Book so if you are struggling with the Student Book questions, try some of the ones in here and then go back to the Student Book – they might suddenly seem easier!

Write your answer in the book to keep questions, answers and your working in one place

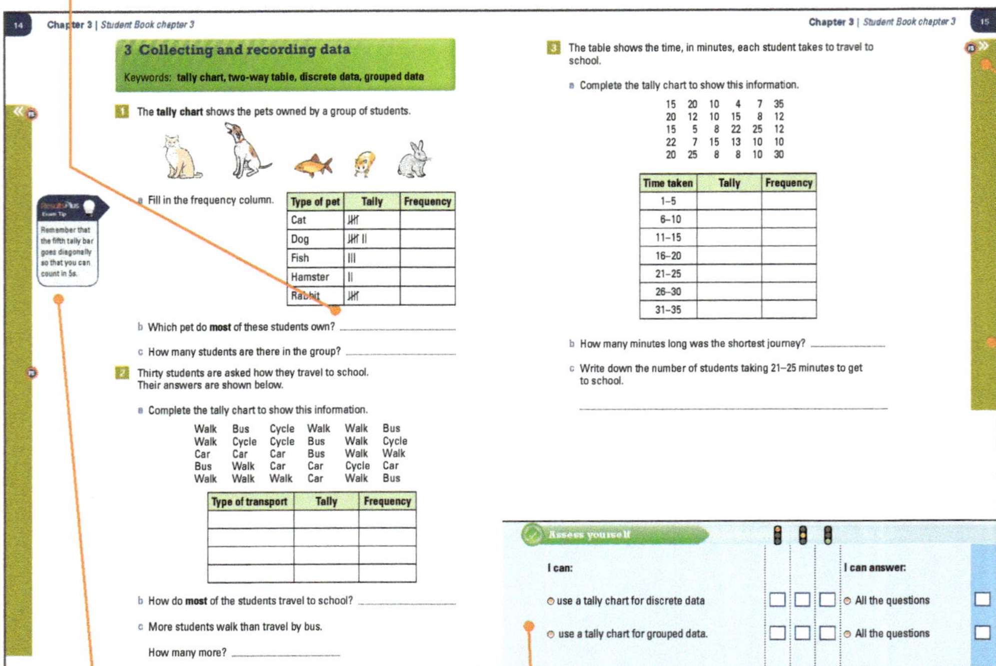

AO2, AO3 and Functional Mathematics questions are labelled – you'll need to answer these in your exam too

Questions are levelled so you can work your way up from one to three arrow questions

ResultsPlus boxes give you handy hints

Assess Yourself boxes so you can keep track of how you are doing

Calculators

You should not use a calculator for any question in this book unless it is marked with a calculator icon like this one

Answers

Your teacher can access the answers at www.edexcelmaths.com/supportplus They will need to register and we will check that they are a teacher before giving them access to the answers! They may choose to give you the answers to mark your own work or they may mark it for you.

About this book

Assessment objectives

Examiners want you to show different skills in the exam and they use **Assessment Objectives** to explain what these are. In the exam, you won't know which question is testing which assessment objective but we've marked them so that you can see how you are doing at each.

45–55% of the marks in your exam will be for AO1 questions which ask you to remember and use the maths you have learned. AO1 questions in this book have no icon on the level bar.

AO2

25–35% of the marks will be for AO2 questions which ask you to choose a way to solve a problem – there may be more than one way.

AO3

15–25% of the marks will be for AO3 questions which ask you to solve a problem and explain how you have solved it.

AO2 or AO3 questions are not more difficult, they just ask you to do something different.

Functional mathematics

FS

30–40% of marks in the Foundation paper are for answering **functional mathematics** questions. These are questions about maths in everyday, real life situations. Again they will not be identified in the exam but we've shown them here so you can see what they are.

Quality of Written Communication

There are also marks available for Quality of Written Communication. This means showing clearly how you got to your answer. These questions are marked with a star (*) in the exam and in this book.

You will need to use the correct maths language and organise the information that you are giving in a logical way to get these marks. As you write into this book, quite often it gives you the structure of the answer and you fill in the gaps. That means that not many questions in this book are marked with a star but look at how some of the others guide you to the answer – you might get some tips for laying out your own work.

Contents

1 Number

Keywords: **place value, order of size, round, multiples, even numbers, odd numbers, factors, negative**

1 Complete the following:

a

$3 \times 2p =$ .... p

b

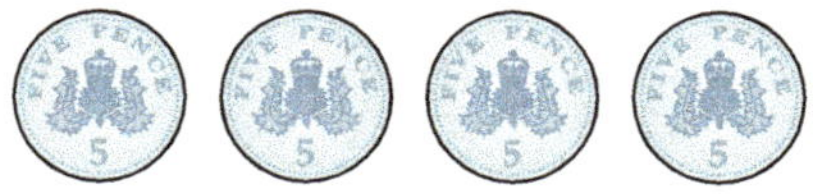

$4 \times 5p =$ .... p

2 Sweets cost 4p each.

How much do 6 sweets cost? .... p

3 **a** On the grid shade all the numbers in the 5 times table.

b On the same grid, shade all the numbers in the 7 times table.
Use a different colour.

1	2	3	4	5	6	7	8	9	10
11	12	13	14	15	16	17	18	19	20
21	22	23	24	25	26	27	28	29	30
31	32	33	34	35	36	37	38	39	40
41	42	43	44	45	46	47	48	49	50
51	52	53	54	55	56	57	58	59	60
61	62	63	64	65	66	67	68	69	70
71	72	73	74	75	76	77	78	79	80
81	82	83	84	85	86	87	88	89	90
91	92	93	94	95	96	97	98	99	100

4 Use this multiplication grid to complete the following

a $8 \times 2 =$ ....

b $7 \times 7 =$ ....

×	**1**	**2**	**3**	**4**	**5**	**6**	**7**	**8**	**9**	**10**
1	1	2	3	4	5	6	7	8	9	10
2	2	4	6	8	10	12	14	16	18	20
3	3	6	9	12	15	18	21	24	27	30
4	4	8	12	16	20	24	28	32	36	40
5	5	10	15	20	25	30	35	40	45	50
6	6	12	18	24	30	36	42	48	54	60
7	7	14	21	28	35	42	49	56	63	70
8	8	16	24	32	40	48	56	64	72	80
9	9	18	27	36	45	54	63	72	81	90
10	10	20	30	40	50	60	70	80	90	100

5 Fill in each missing number.

a .... $\times 7 = 14$ b .... $\times 3 = 36$ c $9 \times$ .... $= 90$

6 A CD costs three pounds, forty-five pence.

Write three pounds, forty-five pence in figures. £ ....

7 The height of Berlin's tallest building is 365 metres.

Write **365** in words. ....

8 Write these numbers in the Hundreds, Tens and Units columns to show their **place values**.

572 45 8 91

H	T	U

9 Write the numbers

17, 34, 285, 140, 6, 99

in **order of size**. Start with the smallest number.

....

10 The table shows the number of people living in four villages.

Blicton	Flindon	Welbury	Yatesville
260	172	93	108

a Which village has the smallest number of people? ....

b Which village has the largest number of people? ....

11 Here are some prices.
Write each price to the nearest pound (£).

Fleece	Boots	Trousers	Shirt
	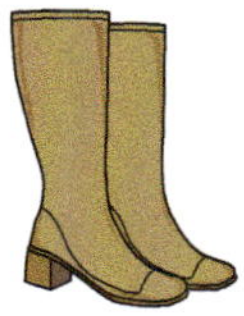	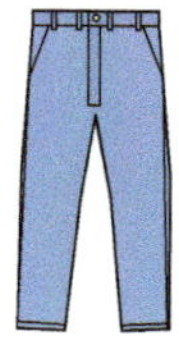	
£14.99	£49.99	£19.99	£14.49

£ .... £ .... £ .... £ ....

12 There are 13 people at a bus stop.
Eight more people come to the bus stop.

AO2 FS

How many people are there at the bus stop now? ....

13 There are 38 books on a shelf in a book shop.
The shop sells 21 of the books.

AO2 FS

How many books are there on the shelf now? ....

14 176 people go to a concert in a school hall.
People sit on rows of chairs. There are 10 chairs in each row.

AO3 FS

How many rows will be needed? ....

15 The table shows the temperature at midnight on 1st January in five cities.

Belfast	London	York	Cardiff	Glasgow
−1°C	5°C	2°C	3°C	−4°C

Write these temperatures in order.
Start with the lowest temperature.

....

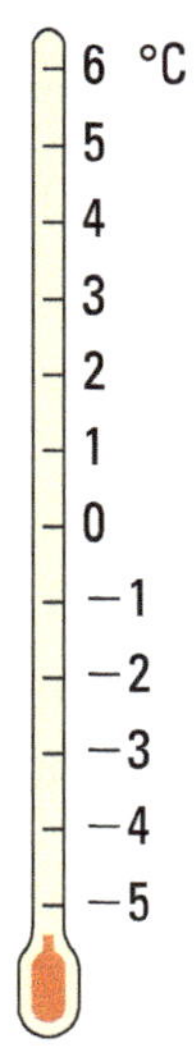

16 The **multiples** of a number are the numbers in its times table.

a Write down the first five multiples of 6

....

....

....

....

....

b Write down the first five multiples of 9

....

....

....

....

....

17 Here is a list of numbers.

2 4 5 8 10 16 20 32 40

Write down the numbers that

a are multiples of 4 ....

b are multiples of 10 ....

18 Write down all the multiples of 3 between 10 and 20

....

19 Write down the next five **even numbers**.

12, 14, 16, 18, 20, 22, ..., ..., ..., ..., ...

20 Write down the **odd numbers** between 190 and 210.

....

21 From the numbers in the cloud, write down

a the even numbers ....

b the odd numbers. ....

22 Here is a list of numbers.

1 2 3 4 5 6 7 8 9 10

Circle all the **factors** of 50.

23 Blackpool Tower is 158 m tall.

Round 158 m to the nearest 10 m. .... m

24 The temperature in Paris is 3°C.
The temperature goes down by 4°C.

Work out the new temperature. .... °C

Assess yourself

I can:	Red	Amber	Green	I can answer:	
find the multiples of a number	☐	☐	☐	Questions 1 to 4, 16 to 18	☐
find the factors of a number	☐	☐	☐	Questions 5, 22	☐
understand and write down whole numbers in figures and in words	☐	☐	☐	Questions 6 to 8	☐
put numbers in order of size	☐	☐	☐	Questions 9 to 10	☐
round numbers	☐	☐	☐	Questions 11 and 23	☐
solve problems using whole numbers	☐	☐	☐	Questions 12 to14	☐
understand and use **negative** numbers.	☐	☐	☐	Questions 15, 24	☐
recognise and write down odd and even numbers.	☐	☐	☐	Questions 19 to 21	☐

2 Angles 1

Keywords: **acute, obtuse, reflex, angle, isosceles, equilateral, right angle, triangle**

«

1 What fraction of a whole turn is each of these **angles**?

a 

.... of a turn

b 

.... of a turn

c 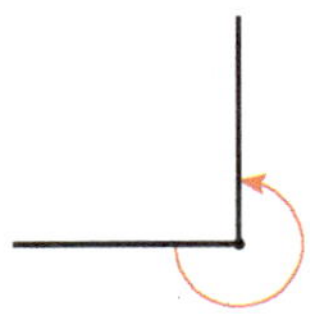

.... of a turn

d 

.... of a turn

2 a Claire is looking north.
She makes a quarter turn clockwise.

What direction is she looking in now? ....

b Peter is looking north and Simon is looking south.
Peter turns to look in the same direction as Simon.

What fraction of a turn does Peter make?

....

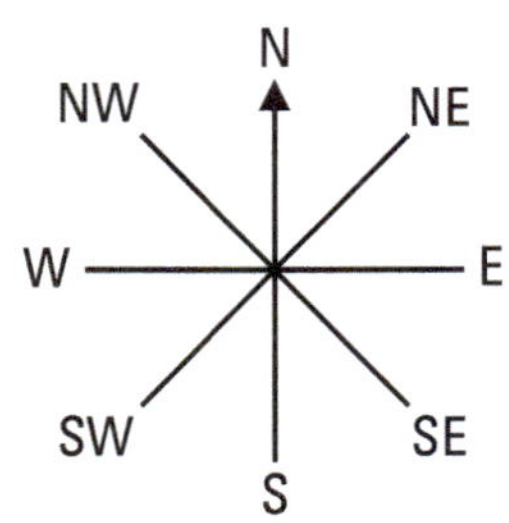

c Mary is looking east.
She makes a quarter turn clockwise.

What direction is Mary looking in now? ....

d Jill is looking north-west.
She makes a half a turn.

What direction is she looking in now? ....

3 Put these angles in order of size.
Start with the smallest angle.

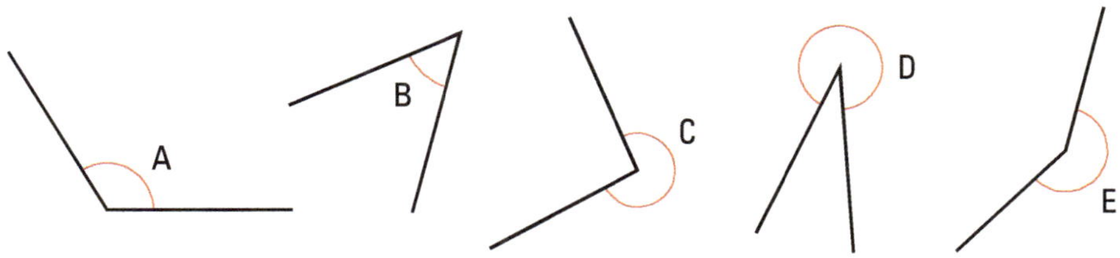

.............., ..., ..., ..., ...

4 **a** Put a circle round the **right-angled triangle**.

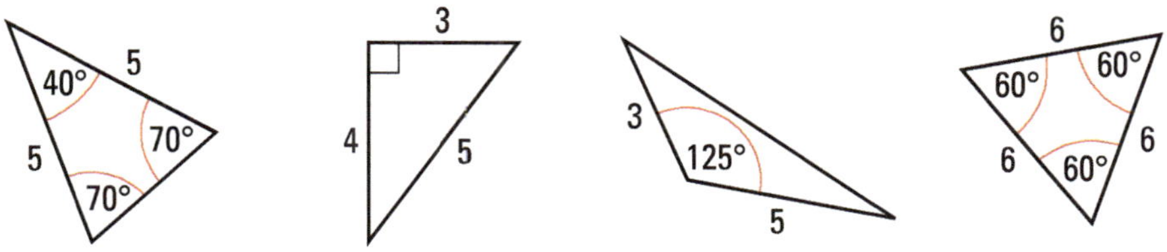

b Two of these triangles are **isosceles**.
Put a circle round each of them.

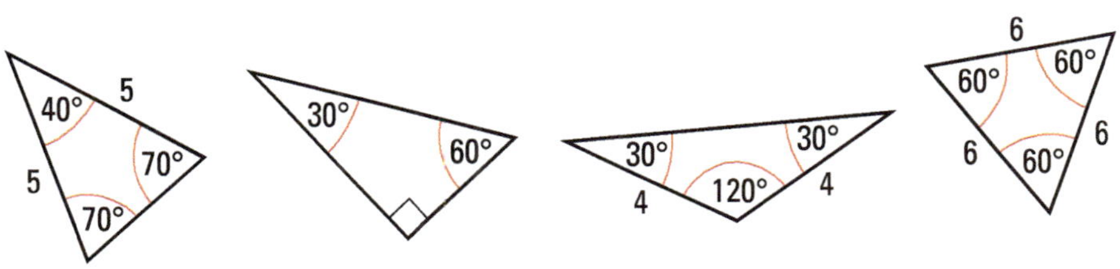

c Put a circle round the **equilateral** triangle.

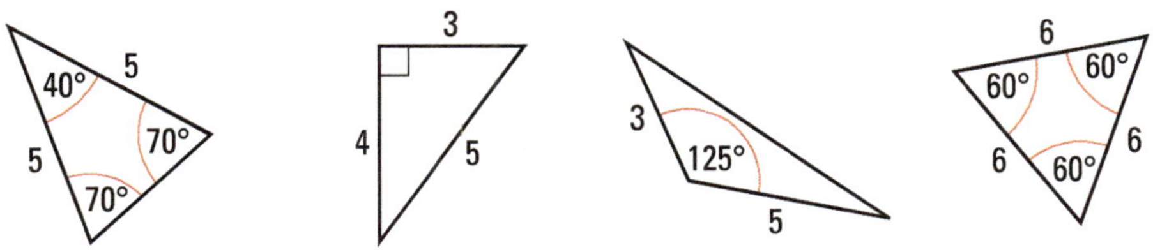

5 Match each angle to its special name.
The first one has been done for you.

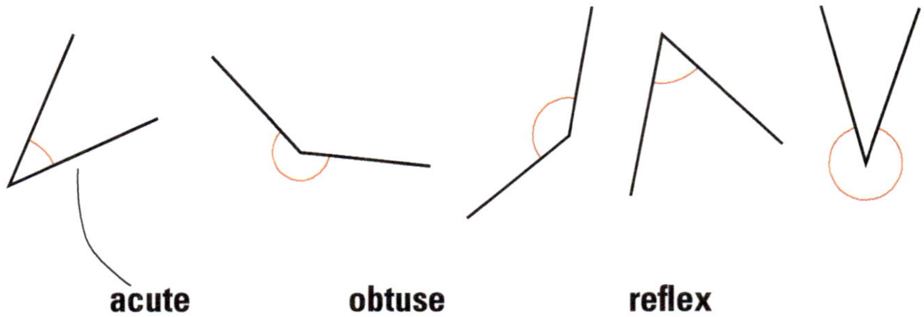

6 Estimate the size of each of these angles.

ResultsPlus Exam Tip

Use the size of angles you know, such as a **right angle**, to help you to estimate the size of angles.

a

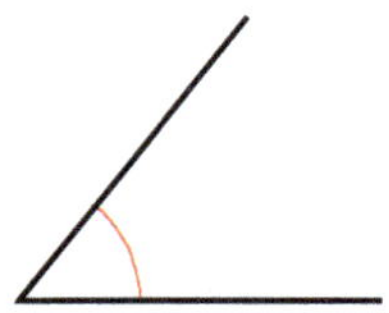

b

c

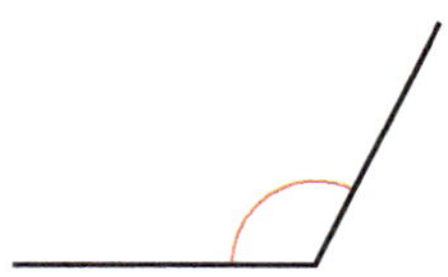

d

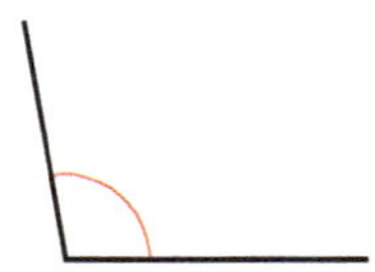

7 Use a protractor to measure the size of these angles.

ResultsPlus Exam Tip

Estimate the size of the angle first. Then remember to line the protractor up carefully and to use the correct scale.

a

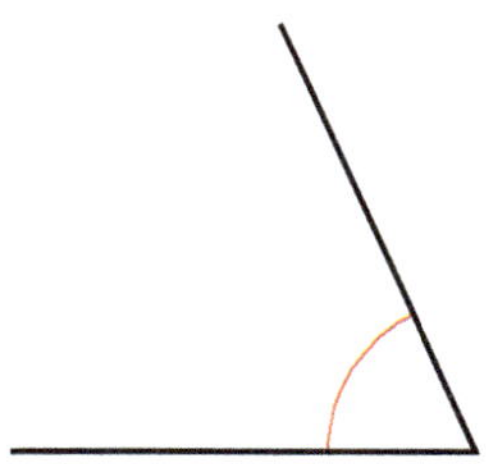

b

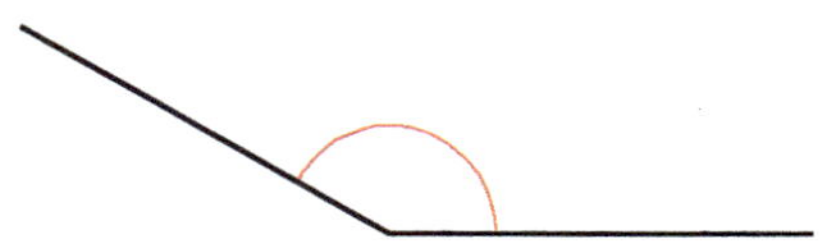

8 Use a protractor to draw the following angles in the space below:

a 70°

b 168°

Assess yourself

I can:				I can answer:	
understand that an angle is a fraction of a turn and use this to answer questions with compass directions	☐	☐	☐	Questions 1 to 2	☐
order angles according to size	☐	☐	☐	Question 3	☐
identify different types of triangle	☐	☐	☐	Question 4	☐
recognise acute, obtuse and reflex angles	☐	☐	☐	Question 5	☐
estimate the size of an angle	☐	☐	☐	Question 6	☐
measure and draw angles.	☐	☐	☐	Questions 7 to 8	☐

3 Collecting and recording data

Keywords: **tally chart, two-way table, discrete data, grouped data**

1 The **tally chart** shows the pets owned by a group of students.

a Fill in the frequency column.

Type of pet	Tally	Frequency
Cat	𝍸	
Dog	𝍸 ||	
Fish	|||	
Hamster	||	
Rabbit	𝍸	

ResultsPlus
Exam Tip

Remember that the fifth tally bar goes diagonally so that you can count in 5s.

b Which pet do **most** of these students own? ....

c How many students are there in the group? ....

2 Thirty students are asked how they travel to school.
Their answers are shown below.

a Complete the tally chart to show this information.

Walk	Bus	Cycle	Walk	Walk	Bus
Walk	Cycle	Cycle	Bus	Walk	Cycle
Car	Car	Car	Bus	Walk	Walk
Bus	Walk	Car	Car	Cycle	Car
Walk	Walk	Walk	Car	Walk	Bus

Type of transport	Tally	Frequency

b How do **most** of the students travel to school? ....

c More students walk than travel by bus.

How many more? ....

3 The table shows the time, in minutes, each student takes to travel to school.

a Complete the tally chart to show this information.

15	20	10	4	7	35
20	12	10	15	8	12
15	5	8	22	25	12
22	7	15	13	10	10
20	25	8	8	10	30

Time taken	Tally	Frequency
1–5		
6–10		
11–15		
16–20		
21–25		
26–30		
31–35		

b How many minutes long was the shortest journey? ....

c Write down the number of students taking 21–25 minutes to get to school.

....

Assess yourself

I can:				**I can answer:**	
use a tally chart for discrete data	☐	☐	☐	All the questions	☐
use a tally chart for grouped data.	☐	☐	☐	All the questions	☐

4 Algebra 1

Keywords: **expression**

1 Jade has 6 pieces of chocolate.
She eats 2 pieces.

How many pieces of chocolate does Jade have now?

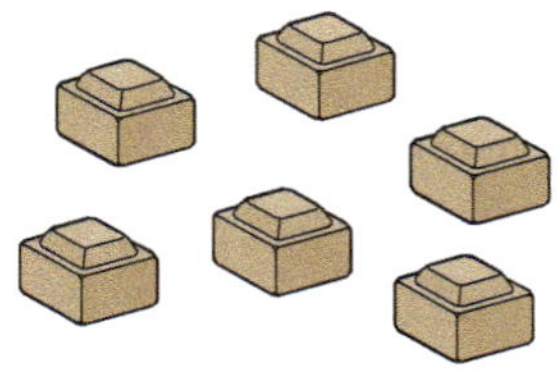

.... pieces

2 Tom has 2 pens.
He buys 3 more.

How many pens does he have now?

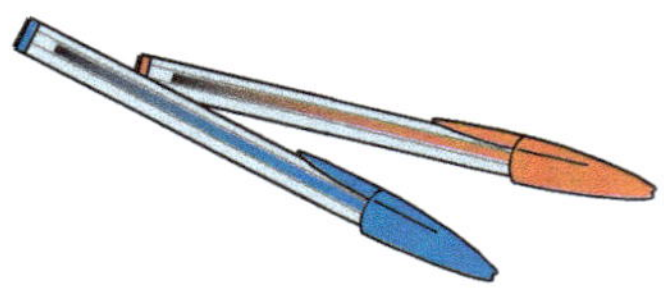

.... pens

3  = ... cars

4  = ... buses

Simplify each **expression** below.

5 $c + c + c = $ ....

6 $b + b + b + b + b = $ ....

7 $p + p + p - p = $ ....

8 $3x + 2x = $ ....

9 $5y - 3y = $ ....

10 $2 \times 3z = $ ....

11 Draw an arrow linking one statement on the left with one **expression** on the right.
One is done for you.

Statement	**Expression**
Add 6 to x	$6x$
Take 6 from x	$x - y$
Multiply x by 6	$x + y$
Take x away from 6	$x + 6$
Add x to y	$x - 6$
Subtract y from x	$6 - x$

12 Becca has k books.
She buys 4 more books.

How many books has Becca got now?

.... books

13 Usma has p plums.
She eats 3 of the plums.

How many plums has Usma got now?

.... plums

14 There are 6 eggs in a box of eggs.
Lewis buys e boxes of eggs.

How many eggs does he buy?

.... eggs

Assess yourself

I can:				**I can answer:**	
collect like terms	☐	☐	☐	Questions 1 to 10	☐
write expressions from information given in different ways.	☐	☐	☐	Questions 11 to 14	☐

5 Decimals and rounding

Keywords: **place value, difference**

1 Write 135 pence in pounds. £ ....

2 Complete the following table.

Measurement	Number of digits	Number of decimal places
24.2	3	1
35.8		1
6.95	3	2
10.375		
287.5		
51.02		

3 Write these numbers in the **place value** diagram.

16.75 2.5 4.99 0.3 8

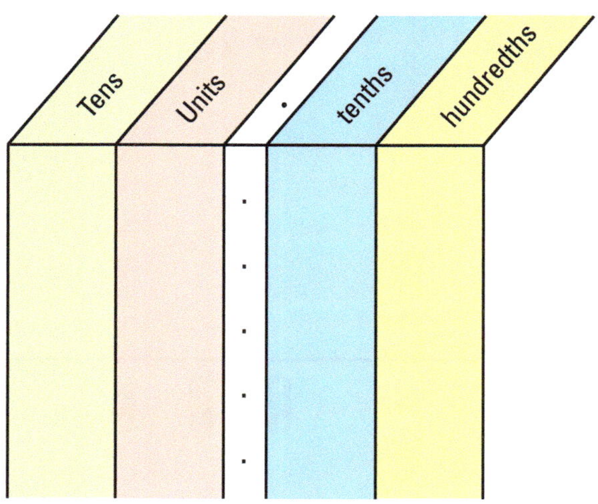

4 Put a circle round each of the numbers that are smaller than 1.

23.6 0.75 1.8 0.04 0.9

5 Write down the reading shown on these scales.
Give your answer to the nearest whole number.

a

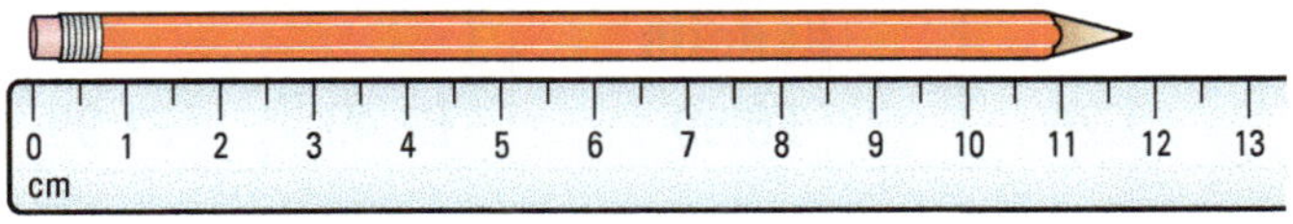

.... cm

b

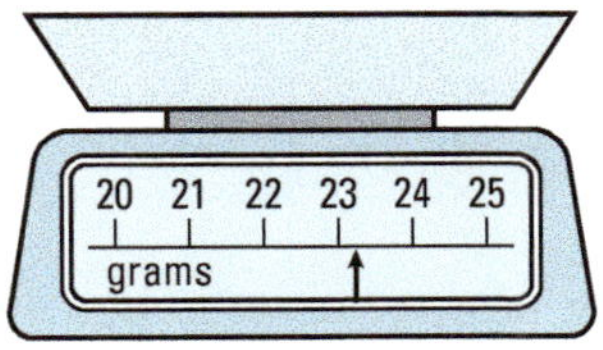

.... g

c

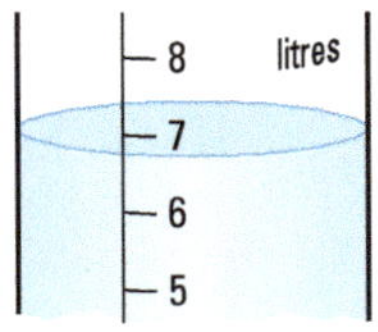

.... *l*

d

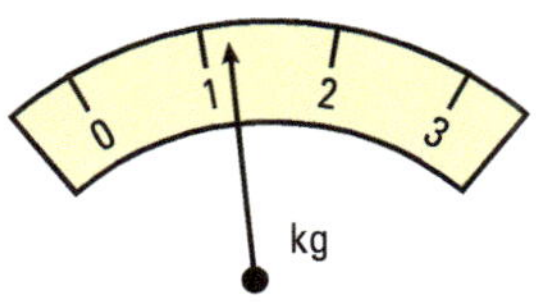

.... kg

e

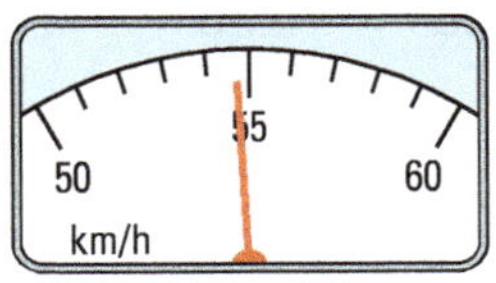

.... km/h

6 Complete the following bill.

Packet of crisps	£0.62
Bar of chocolate	£0.79
Bottle of water	£0.45
	£

A02

FS

7 **a** Work out 2.5 g + 1.8 g .... g

b Work out £3.50 − £2.38 £ ....

c Work out 3 × 1.50 m .... m

d Work out £1.76 ÷ 2 £ ....

«

A02

FS

8 The table shows the costs of some things sold in a school shop.

Pencil case	Ruler	Maths set	Set of colouring pencils	Gel pen	Protractor
£3.49	£3.49	£1.25	£6.99	£7.49	£1.99

a Which is the cheapest? ....

b Work out the total cost of one maths set and one pencil case.

....

«‹

9 Write these numbers in order of size.
Start with the smallest number.

0.5 1.5 0.25 1.25 0.75

....

10 a Round 3.8 cm to the nearest cm. .... cm

b Round 69 m to the nearest 10 m. .... m

c Round £723 to the nearest £100. £ ....

d Round 1925 km to the nearest 1000 km. .... km

e Round 4 h 50 min to the nearest hour. .... hours

11 There are 21 739 people at a football match.

Round **21 739** to the nearest thousand. ....

12 Peter has to walk 380 m to the bus stop.

Round **380** to the nearest hundred metres. .... m

A02

FS

13 1 tin of dog food costs 41p.

Work out the cost of 12 tins of dog food.
Give your answer in pounds (£).

£ ....

14 In 2007 the world record for running 100 m was 9.74 seconds.
In 2009 Usain Bolt set a new world record of 9.58 seconds.

Work out the **difference** between these two times.

AO2 FS

.... seconds

15 £15.80 is shared equally between four children.

How much money does each child get?

AO2

£ ....

16 Seven people each buy a meal.
Each meal costs £5.95

AO2 AO3 FS

Estimate the total cost. £ ....

Assess yourself

I can:	Red	Amber	Green	I can answer:	
understand place value and compare the size of decimal numbers	☐	☐	☐	Questions 1, 3 to 4, 9	☐
understand the difference between the number of digits and the number of decimal places	☐	☐	☐	Question 2	☐
round numbers	☐	☐	☐	Questions 5, 10 to 12	☐
add, subtract, multiply and divide decimals	☐	☐	☐	Questions 6 to 7	☐
solve problems using decimals	☐	☐	☐	Questions 8, 13 to 15	☐
estimate answers to calculations without using a calculator.	☐	☐	☐	Question 16	☐

6 Two dimensional shapes

Keywords: **triangle, quadrilateral, line symmetry, rotational symmetry**

A03

FS

ResultsPlus Exam Tip

The triangles are of three different types: isosceles, right-angled and equilateral.

1 i Put a ring round the **triangle** that is the odd one out on each line.
ii Explain why it is different to the others.

a

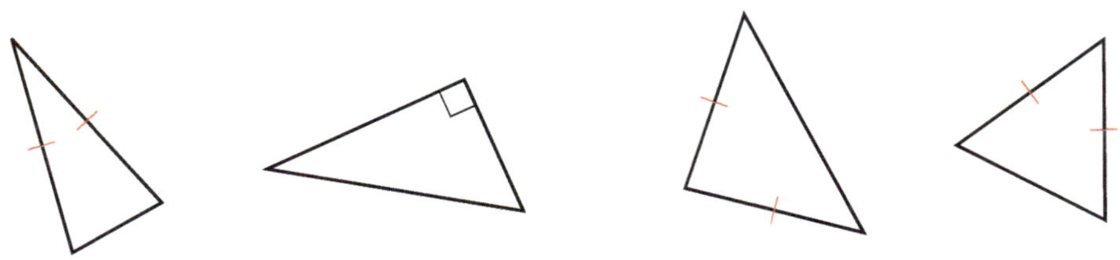

Explanation ....

b

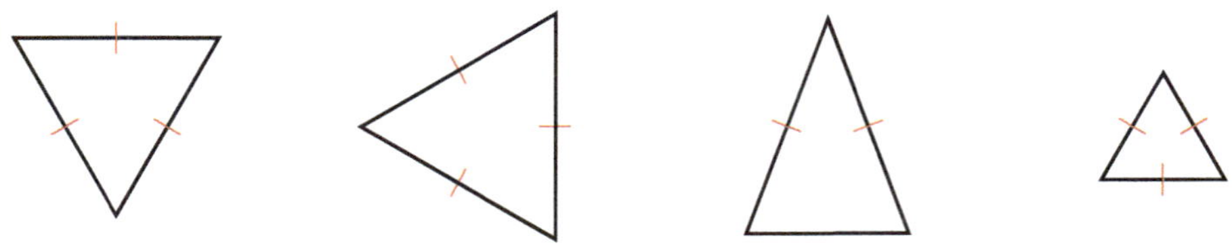

Explanation ....

ResultsPlus Exam Tip

A quadrilateral has four sides. Some examples are: square, rectangle, parallelogram, rhombus and trapezium.

2 In the space below, sketch a shape that matches each description and write its mathematical name.

a A **quadrilateral** with four equal length sides and four right angles.

Name ....

b A quadrilateral with one pair of parallel sides of different lengths. The other two sides are not parallel to each another.

Name ....

c A quadrilateral with four equal length sides but the angles are not right angles.

Name ....

d A quadrilateral with two pairs of opposite equal parallel sides and four right angles.

Name ....

3 a Draw a circle with radius 3 cm.
Use a coloured pencil to show the circumference of the circle.

b i Draw a circle with diameter 7 cm.

ii Draw a radius on the circle.

iii Measure the length of this radius.

iv Write this length on your radius.

c i Draw a circle with radius 3 cm. Use × as the centre.

×

ii Use the same centre (×) to draw a circle with radius 4 cm.

4 Complete each drawing so that it has **line symmetry**.

a
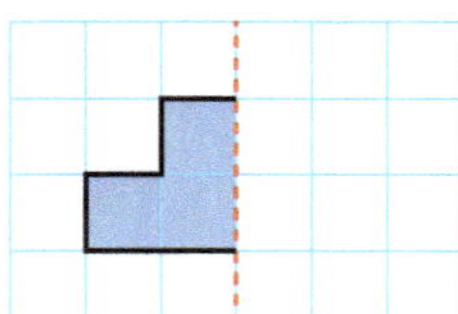

b
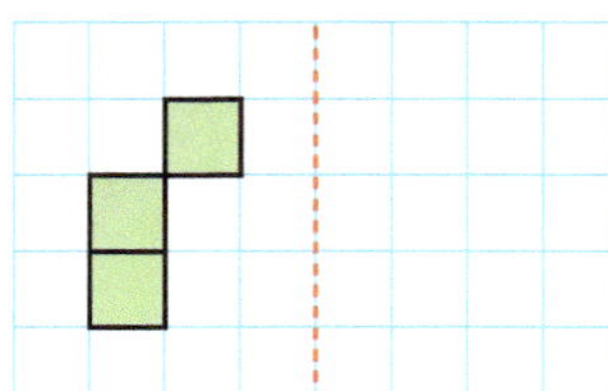

c
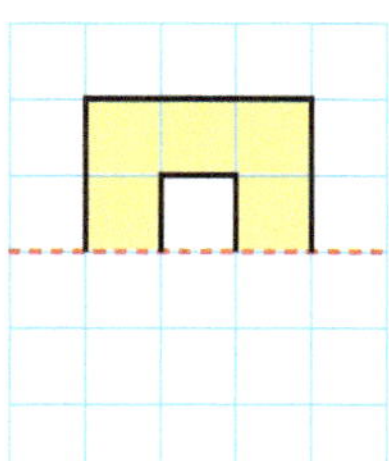

d
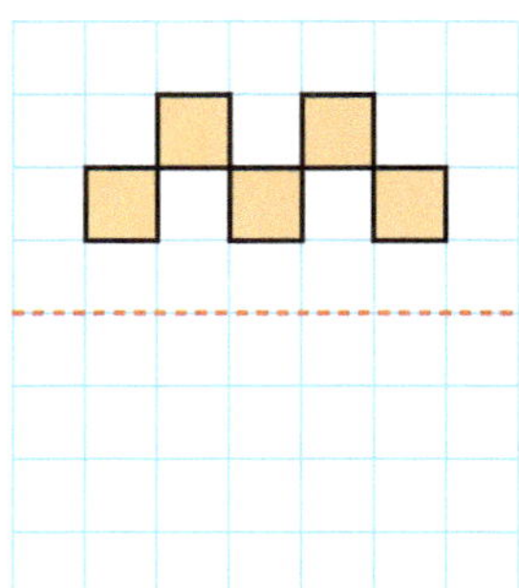

5 Complete each drawing so that it has line symmetry.

a
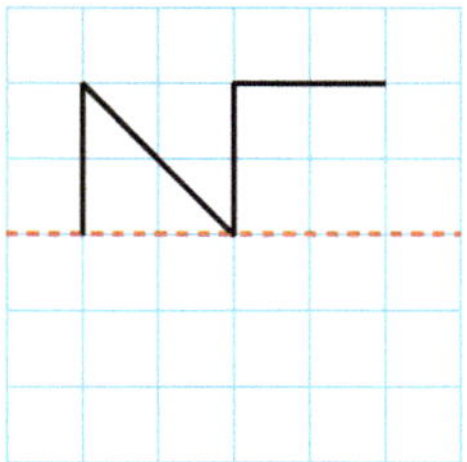

b

c
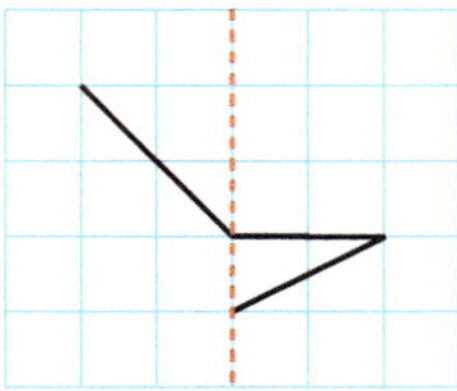

d
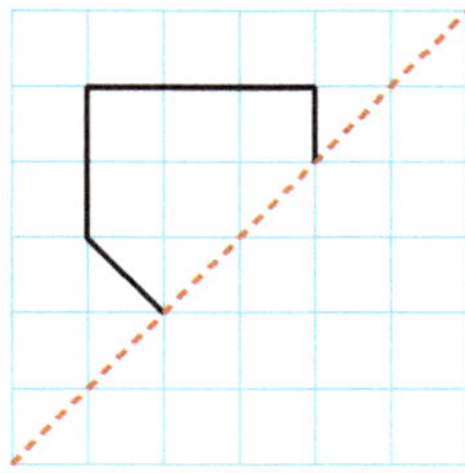

6 Write the order of rotation underneath each picture.

a

....

b

....

c

....

ResultsPlus
Exam Tip

To see if a shape has **rotational symmetry**, rotate it one full turn. See how many times the shape still looks the same.

Assess yourself

I can:				I can answer:	
recognise different types of triangles	☐	☐	☐	Question 1	☐
recognise different types of quadrilateral	☐	☐	☐	Question 2	☐
draw a circle and label its parts	☐	☐	☐	Question 3	☐
draw the reflection of a shape in a mirror line	☐	☐	☐	Questions 4 to 5	☐
give the order of rotation of a shape.	☐	☐	☐	Question 6	☐

7 Angles 2

Keywords: **parallel, perpendicular**

1 Draw lines to match the shapes to their mathematical names.

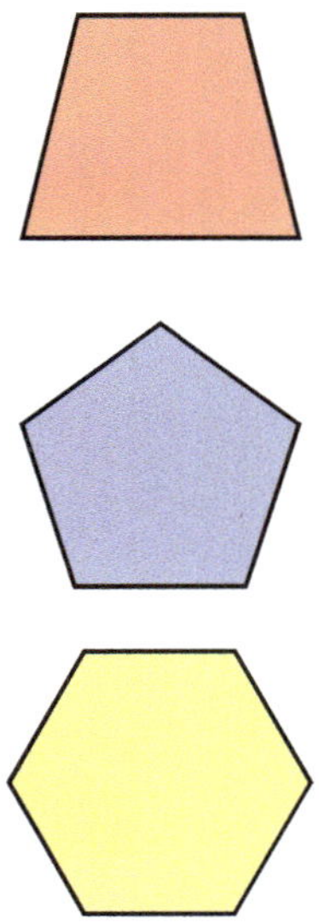

parallelogram

hexagon

pentagon

trapezium

octagon

rectangle

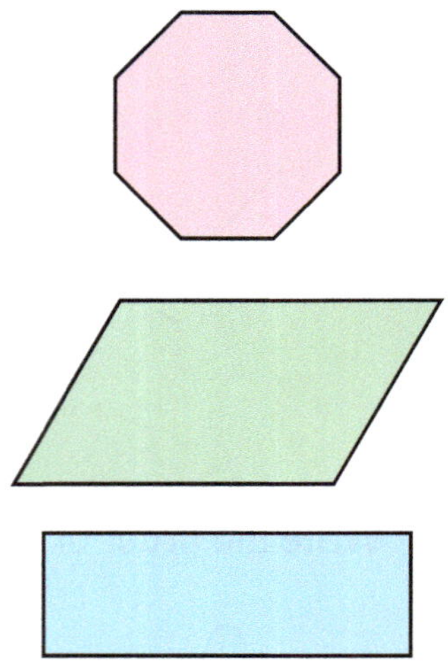

2 Use a coloured pen or pencil to show the **parallel** lines in the diagrams. Use a different colour for each set of parallel lines you find.

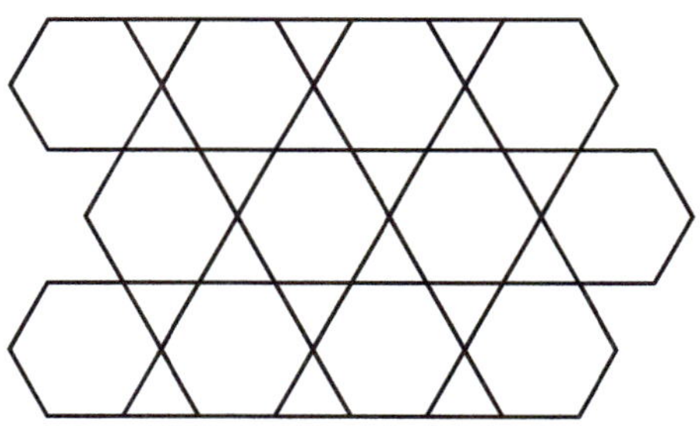

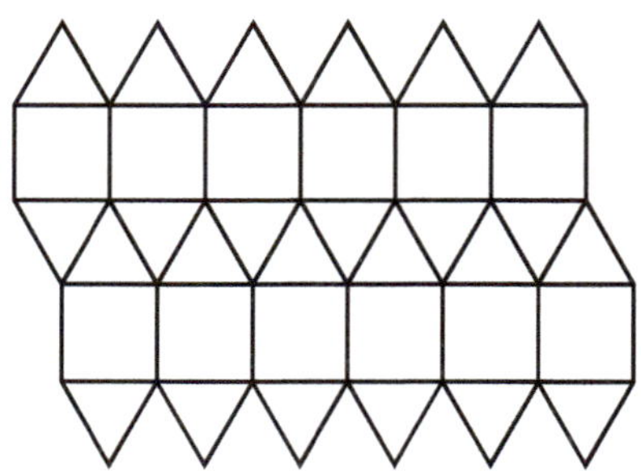

ResultsPlus Exam Tip

Parallel lines remain the same distance apart and never cross.

3 Use a coloured pen or pencil to show the **perpendicular** lines in the diagrams. Use a different colour for each set of perpendicular lines you find.

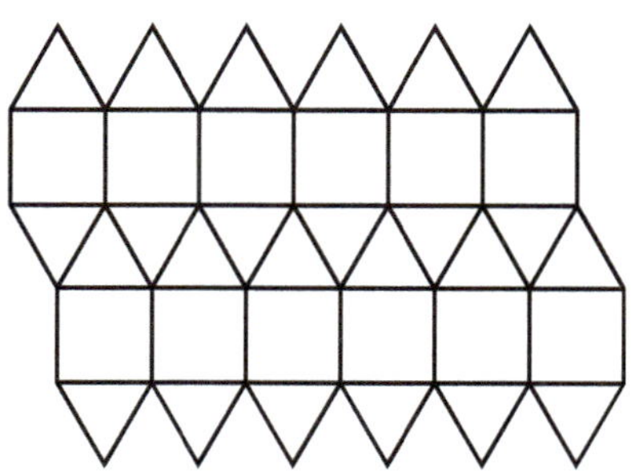

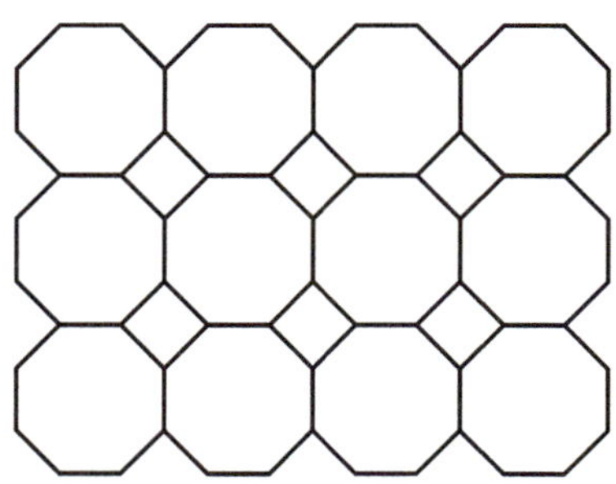

ResultsPlus Exam Tip

Perpendicular lines meet at a 90° angle.

4 This is an accurately drawn quadrilateral.

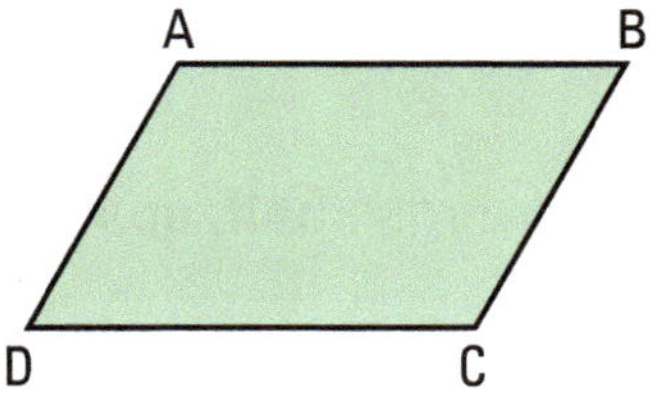

a Write down the mathematical name for the quadrilateral.

....

b Which side is parallel to AB? ....

c Which side is parallel to AD? ....

5 These diagrams have not been drawn to scale.
Calculate the size of the marked angles.
The first two have been done for you.

a

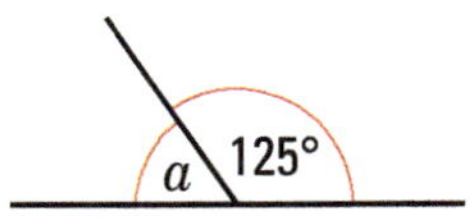

$a + 125° = 180°$
$a = 180° - 125°$
$a = 55°$

b

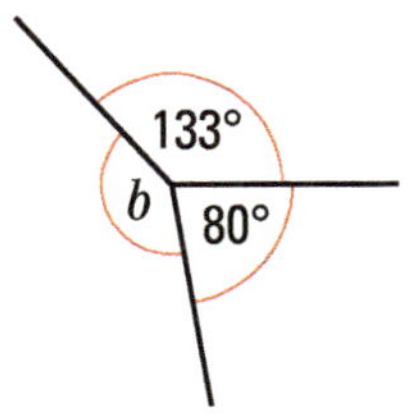

$133° + 80° + b = 360°$
$b = 360° - 133° - 80°$
$b = 147°$

c

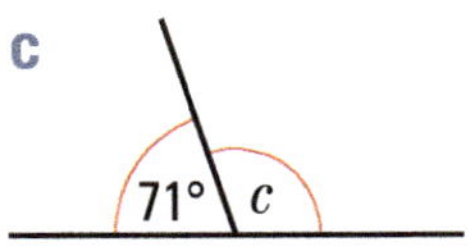

....

....

....

d

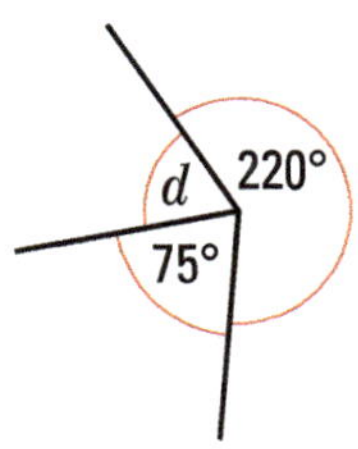

....

....

....

ResultsPlus Exam Tip

Remember that angles on a straight line add to 180° and angles round a point add to 360°. If diagrams are not drawn to scale you cannot measure them to find the size of the angles, you need to do a calculation.

Assess yourself

I can:				I can answer:	
recognise and name shapes	☐	☐	☐	Question 1	☐
understand what parallel lines and perpendicular lines are	☐	☐	☐	Questions 2 to 4	☐
use the sum of angles at a point and on a straight line to find missing angles.	☐	☐	☐	Question 5	☐

8 Fractions

Keywords: **half, quarter, third**

1 There are equal numbers of boys and girls in a class.

What fraction of the class are boys? ....

2 Kelly has £20.
She gives £5 to Kathy.

What fraction of the £20 is this? ....

3 Here are some shapes.

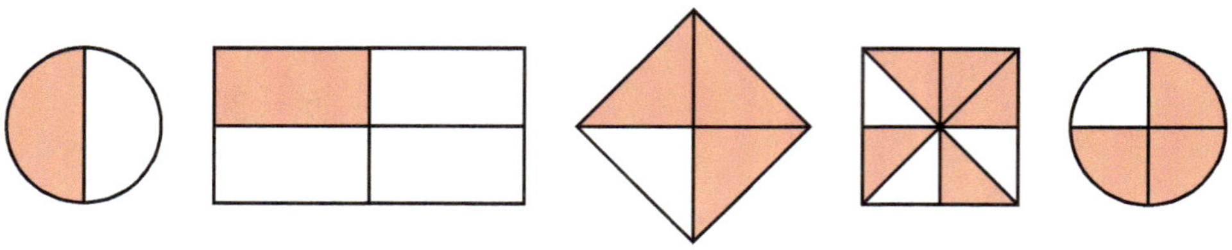

....

Tick the shape that is **half** shaded.

4 **a** Shade $\frac{1}{4}$ of 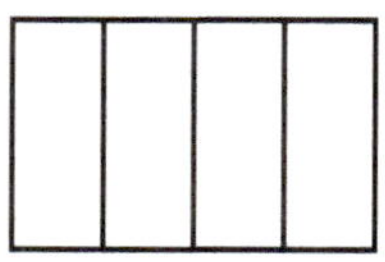

b Shade $\frac{1}{2}$ of 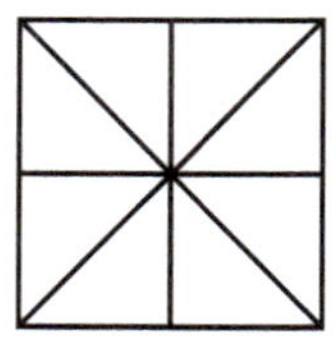

c Shade $\frac{3}{4}$ of 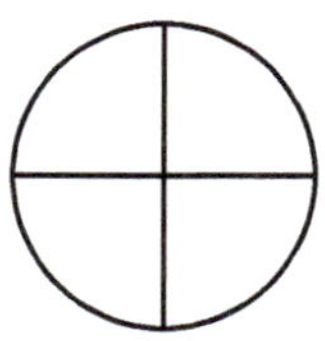

d Shade $\frac{1}{3}$ of 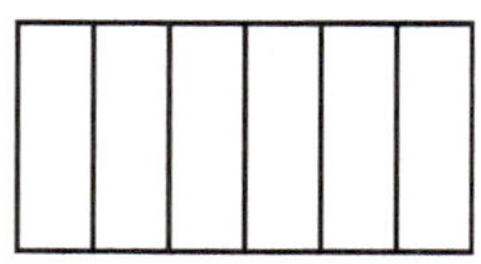

5 There are 8 biscuits in a packet.
Jon eats half of the biscuits.

a How many biscuits does Jon eat? ....

b How many biscuits are there now? ....

6 There are 100 cars in a car park.
One **quarter** of the cars are red.

a How many cars are red? ....

b What fraction of the cars are not red? ....

7 There are 30 students in a maths class.
One **third** of the students have brown eyes.

How many students have brown eyes? ....

8 Work out

A02

a $\frac{1}{2}$ of 12 ....

b $\frac{1}{3}$ of 15 ....

c $\frac{1}{4}$ of 8 ....

d $\frac{4}{5}$ of 50 ....

e $\frac{1}{10}$ of 80 ....

9 Work out $\frac{2}{5}$ of £20 ....

10 Ben cuts a cake into 8 equal slices.
He gives 3 slices to friends.

What fraction of the cake does Ben have now?

Circle the answer: $\frac{1}{2}$ $\frac{3}{8}$ $\frac{5}{8}$ $\frac{3}{5}$ $\frac{1}{3}$

Assess yourself

I can:				I can answer:	
write one quantity as a fraction of another	☐	☐	☐	Questions 1 to 2, 10	☐
understand fractions	☐	☐	☐	Questions 3 to 4	☐
find fractions of quantities.	☐	☐	☐	Questions 5 to 9	☐

9 Algebra 2

Keywords: **expression, power**

1 Work out the distance between A and C.

.... cm

2 Work out the distance between M and N.

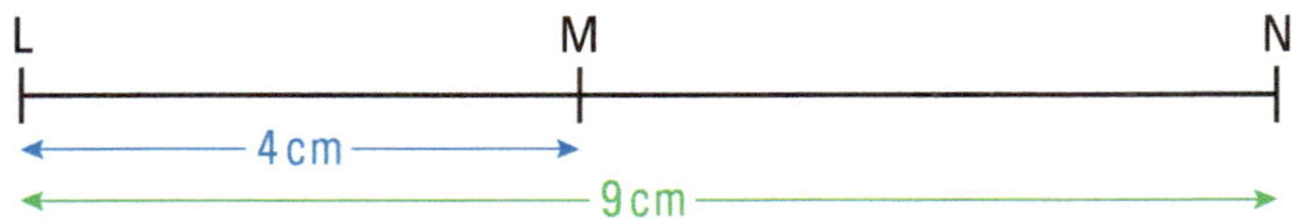

.... cm

3 Write down an **expression** for the distance between P and R.

....

4 Write down an expression for the distance between S and T.

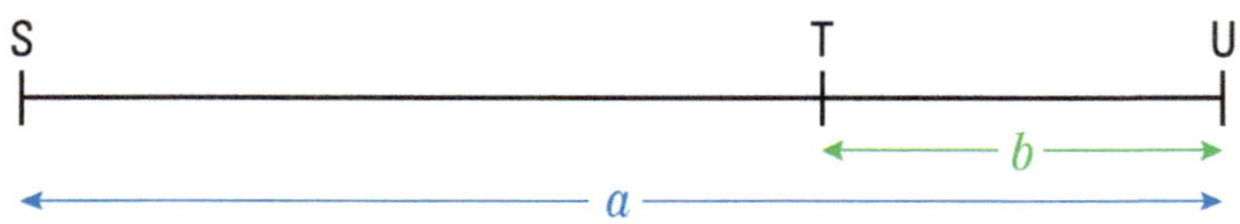

....

5 Simplify each expression.

a $2 \times a$ = ...

b $3 \times b$ = ...

c $c \times 5$ = ...

d $3 \times 2d$ = ...

e $e + e + e + e$ = ...

6 Fill in the table below to show the first five **powers** of 2.

$2^1 =$	2	$= 2$
$2^2 =$	2×2	$= 4$
$2^3 =$	$2 \times 2 \times 2$	$= 8$
$2^4 =$		$=$
$2^5 =$		$= 32$

7 Fill in the table below to show the first two **powers** of 3.

$3^1 =$	3	$= 3$
$3^2 =$	3×3	$=$

8 Draw lines to link the expression in the top row with its value in the bottom row.

One has been done for you.

5^2 3^2 2^2 9^2 8^2 6^2

36 25 9 4 81 64

Assess yourself

I can:				I can answer:	
write expressions using algebra	☐	☐	☐	Questions 1 to 4	☐
simplify expressions	☐	☐	☐	Question 5	☐
work out the value of numbers to a power.	☐	☐	☐	Questions 6 to 8	☐

10 Using a calculator

Keywords: **calculator, numerator, denominator**

Use your **calculator** to answer all the questions.
Give all your answers as whole numbers or decimals, **not** as fractions.

1 Work out

a 57 + 28 ....

b 83 − 46 ....

c 29 × 6 ....

d 408 ÷ 17 ....

2 Find the answers to the following.
Write down all the figures on your calculator display.

a 97.2 × 27 = ...

b 36 ÷ 7 = ...

3 There are 486 male students, 469 female students and 48 teachers in a school.

Work out the total number of students and teachers. ....

4 A shop has 125 newspapers.
It sells 89 of the newspapers.

How many newspapers are left? ....

5 276 people go on a bus trip.
Up to 52 people can go on one bus.

How many buses are needed? ....

6 In Bill's café, a cup of tea costs 38p.

Work out the total cost of 6 cups of tea. ....

7 Chris uses her calculator to work out £84 divided by 8
Her calculator display is shown.

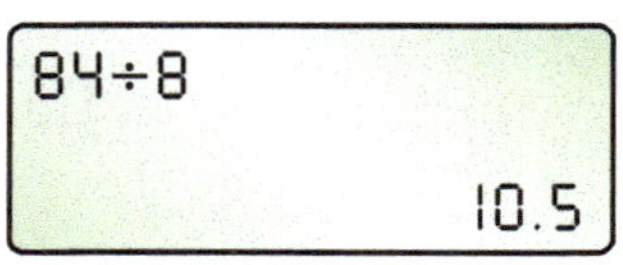

How should Chris write down her answer?
Circle one of these.

10.5 £10.50 10.50 £10.5 10.5p

FS A02

8 a Complete the bill.

Carla's Café	
Tea	85p
Coffee	95p
Squash	70p
Sandwiches	£1.40
Cakes	80p

2 Teas ....

3 Coffees ....

1 Squash ....

1 Sandwich ....

4 Cakes ....

Total £ ________

b Max pays the bill with a £20 note.

How much change should Max get? £ ....

9 To write a fraction as a decimal, divide the **numerator** by the **denominator**.

a Write $\frac{3}{4}$ as a decimal. ....

b Write $\frac{23}{25}$ as a decimal. ....

c Write $\frac{7}{16}$ as a decimal. ....

10 Use the $\boxed{\sqrt{}}$ and $\boxed{x^2}$ buttons on your calculator to work out:

a 9^2 b 16^2 c 2.5^2 d $\sqrt{169}$ e $\sqrt{13.69}$

....

Assess yourself

I can:				I can answer:	
work out calculations	☐	☐	☐	Questions 1 to 2	☐
solve word problems and complete bills	☐	☐	☐	Questions 3 to 8	☐
convert fractions to decimals	☐	☐	☐	Question 9	☐
find squares and square roots.	☐	☐	☐	Question 10	☐

11 Measure

Keywords: **metric measurement, imperial measurement**

1 Change these 12-hour times to 24-hour times:

a 6.15 am ....

b 5.20 pm ....

c 12.15 am ....

FS

2 Change these 24-hour times to 12-hour times:

a 16:40 ....

b 01:30 ....

c 23.35 ....

FS

3 a Sue arrives at school at 8.45 am. She leaves school at 3:10 pm.

How long is she at school?

....

b It takes Sally 12 minutes to type an email.
She has to type 5 emails.

How long will she take?

....

c Faysal gets on a bus at 08:10. He gets off the bus at 08:50.

How long is he on the bus?

....

4 Write down the **metric measurement** you would use to measure the following. Draw lines to match them up.

length of an exercise book	mm
weight of a person	m
length of a long piece of rope	kg
distance from home to the supermarket	g
weight of a bus	cm
weight of a pencil	km
thickness of a £1 coin	tonnes

5 Measure the length of each line.
Give your answers in centimetres and millimetres.

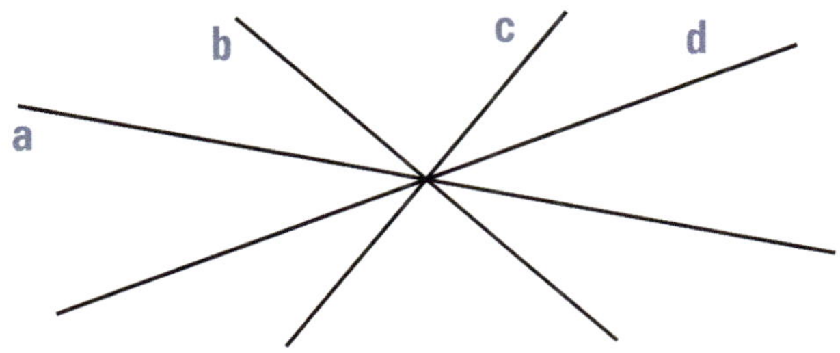

a .... cm
.... mm
b .... cm
.... mm
c .... cm
.... mm
d .... cm
.... mm

6 Write down the readings shown on these scales:

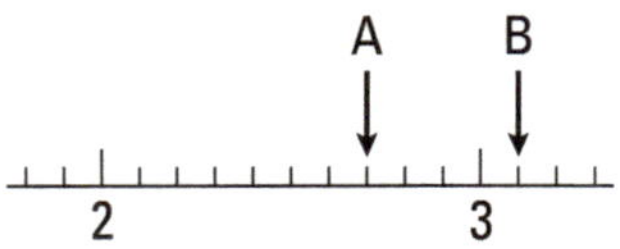

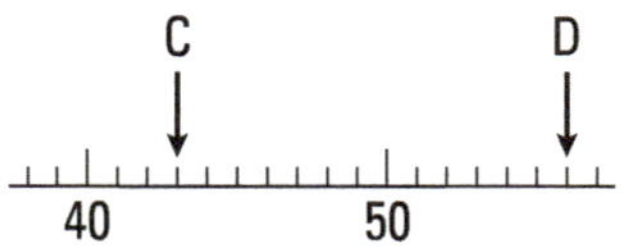

A .... B .... C .... D ....

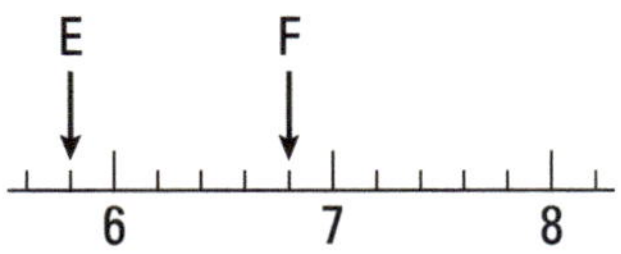

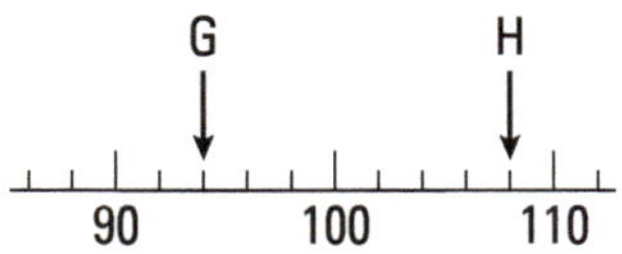

E .... F .... G .... H ....

7 Change the following measurements:

a 7 kilometres into metres

....

b 200 metres into kilometres

....

c 55 centimetres into metres

....

d 70 millimetres into centimetres

....

e 8000 millilitres into litres

....

f 6.5 litres into millilitres

....

g 900 grams into kilograms

....

h 8.67 kilograms into grams

....

FS

8 **a** Susan has a piece of string 5.2 m long.
Sarah has a piece of string 523 cm long.

i Who has the longer piece of string?

....

ii How much longer is it?

....

b My car needs 8 *l* of oil. I buy two 3 *l* cans of oil and two 1500 m*l* cans of oil. I put 8 *l* of oil in my car. How much oil will I have left over?

....

c Simon is making 2 cakes. He needs 125 g of sugar for the first cake.
He needs 280 g of sugar for the second cake.
His 1 kg bag of sugar is only half full.

Does he have enough sugar to make both cakes?

....

9 Draw lines from the boxes in list A to match the metric and **imperial** equivalents. The first has been done for you.
For example, card A goes with card 5.

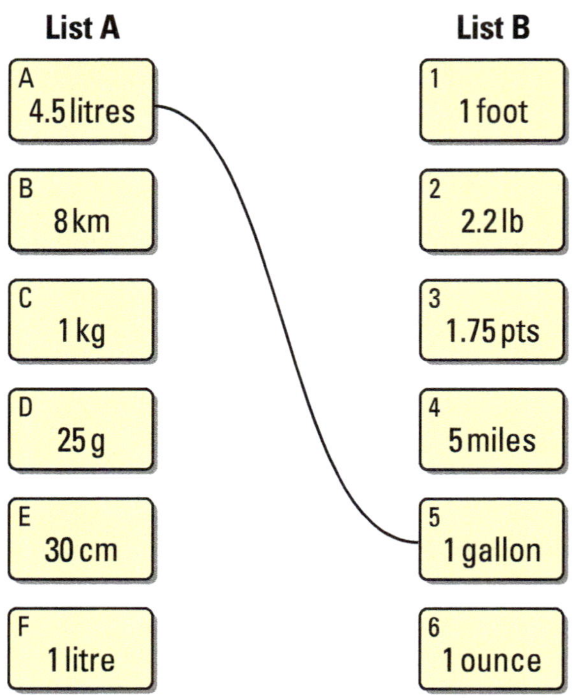

10 a Convert 9 litres into gallons.

....

b Convert 75 g into ounces.

....

c Convert 45 cm into feet.

....

d Jim is baking a cake.
The recipe is in imperial units, but his scales only weigh metric.
The recipe needs 6 ounces of flour.

How many grams of flour does he need?

....

e Ann is making some lemonade.
Her measuring jug measures in litres.
She needs $3\frac{1}{2}$ pints of water.

How many litres does she need to measure out?

....

ResultsPlus Exam Tip

You can use your answers from question 9 to help you.

Assess yourself

I can:	Red	Amber	Green	I can answer:	
convert between 12-hour times and 24-hour times	☐	☐	☐	Questions 1 to 2	☐
calculate with time	☐	☐	☐	Question 3	☐
choose suitable metric units for measuring	☐	☐	☐	Question 4	☐
measure a line accurately to the nearest mm	☐	☐	☐	Question 5	☐
read a scale	☐	☐	☐	Question 6	☐
convert between metric units	☐	☐	☐	Questions 7 to 8	☐
convert between metric and imperial units.	☐	☐	☐	Questions 9 to 10	☐

12 Processing, representing and interpreting data

Keywords: **pictogram, bar chart, pie chart**

1 The table shows the sales of food and drinks in a café one lunchtime.

Food	Number of sales
Tea	7
Coffee	9
Sandwich	4
Fruit	10
Pie	8

Draw a **pictogram** to show this information.

Use ⊖ to represent 2 items.

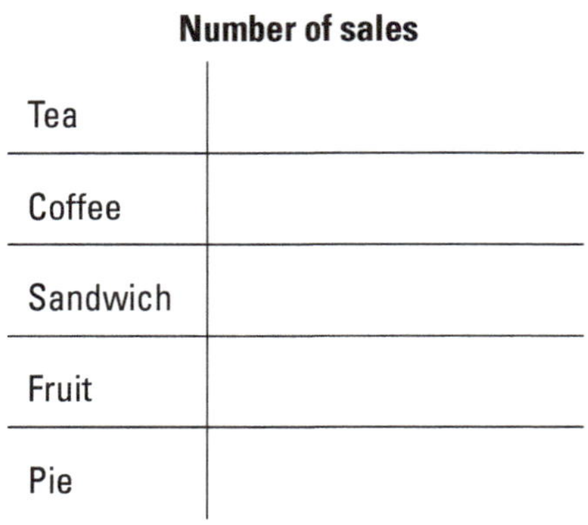

2 The pictogram shows the weather in April.

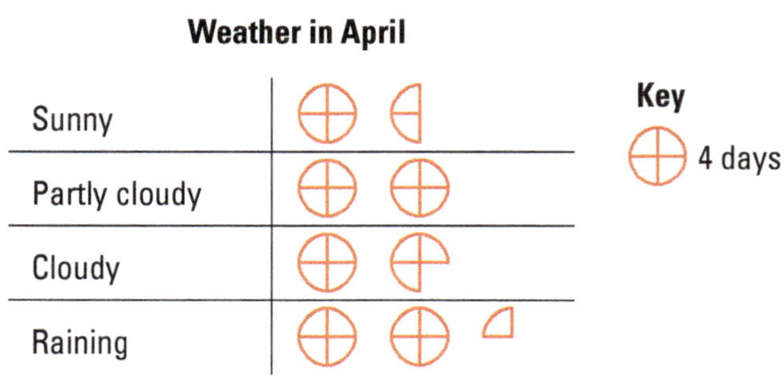

a What was the weather on most days? ....

b On how many days was it raining? ....

c What are the total number of days shown? ....

3 The table shows the number of students that have part time jobs.

Job	Number of students
Paper round	8
Shop work	11
Café or restaurant	7
Other	4
None	9

Draw a **bar chart** to illustrate the data.

ResultsPlus Exam Tip

Remember to use a ruler and pencil. The bars for discrete data do not touch one another. Remember to label the axes as well.

4 The bar chart shows the average number of hours of daily sunshine each day in the months from January to December in Madeira.

A03

FS

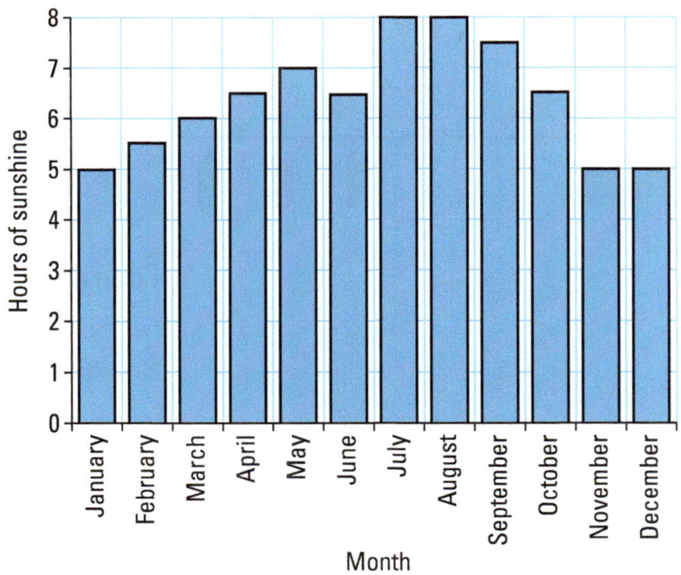

a Which months have the most sunshine?

.... and ....

b How many hours of sunshine each day are there in April? .... hours

5 The **pie chart** shows land use on a farm.

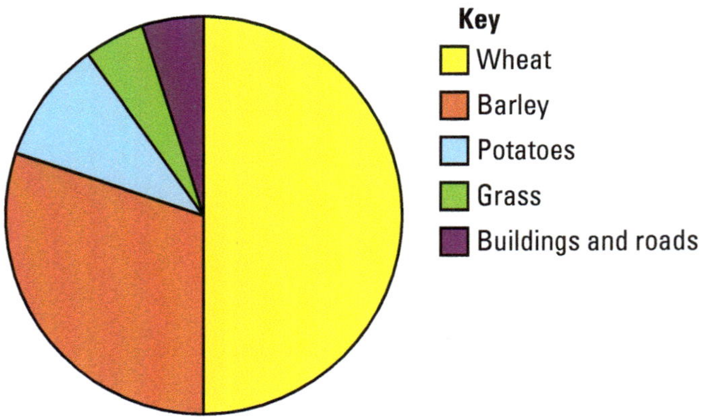

a What is the most land used for? ....

b Estimate the percentage of land that is used for barley.

.... %

c Which two sectors are the same size?

.... and ....

Assess yourself

I can:				I can answer:	
draw a pictogram	☐	☐	☐	Question 1	☐
use a pictogram	☐	☐	☐	Question 2	☐
draw a bar chart	☐	☐	☐	Question 3	☐
use a bar chart	☐	☐	☐	Question 4	☐
use a pie chart.	☐	☐	☐	Question 5	☐

13 Sequences

Keywords: **sequence, pattern**

1 Here is a number **sequence**.

Write down the next three odd numbers in the sequence.

1, 3, 5, 7, 9, ..., ..., ...

2 a Here is a different sequence.

Write down the next three numbers in the sequence.

2, 4, 6, 8, 10, ..., ..., ...

b Fill in the missing word.

The numbers 2, 4, 6, ... are .... numbers.

3 Find the missing numbers in the number **patterns** below.

a 4, 8, 12, 16, ..., ..., 28, 32, ...

b 10, 20, ..., 40, 50, ..., ...

c 1, 6, 11, 16, 21, ..., ..., ...

d 100, 95, 90, 85, 80, ..., ..., ...

4 Start with 7.
To get the next number, add 3 each time.

Write down the first five terms in the sequence.

........., ..., ..., ..., ...

AO2 AO3

5 a Draw the next pattern in the sequence.

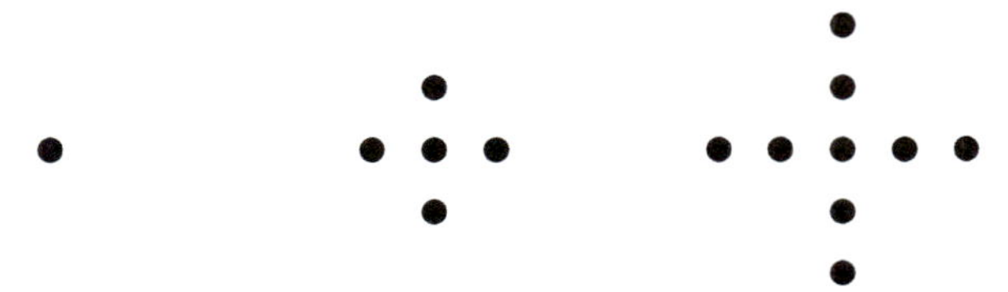

Pattern number 1 | Pattern number 2 | Pattern number 3 | Pattern number 4

b Complete the table.

Pattern number	1	2	3	4	5
Number of dots	1	5			

c How many dots are there in Pattern number 9? ....

AO2 AO3

FS

6 The patterns are made from matchsticks.

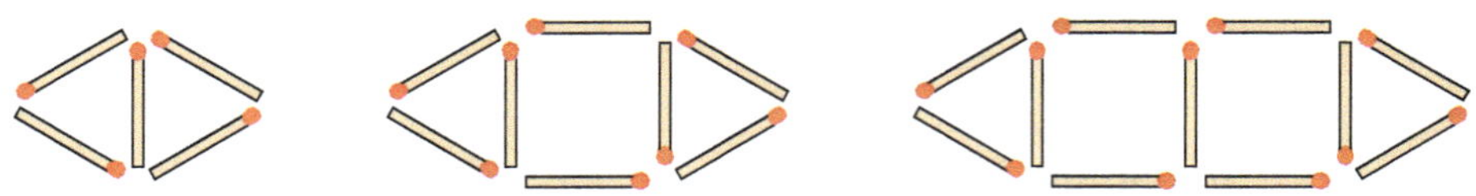

Pattern number 1 | Pattern number 2 | Pattern number 3

a Draw the next pattern in the sequence.

b Complete the table.

Pattern number	1	2	3	4	5
Number of matchsticks	5	8			

c Work out the number of matchsticks needed for Pattern number 10.

....

Assess yourself

I can:				**I can answer:**
write down odd and even numbers	☐	☐	☐	Questions 1 to 2
find the missing numbers in a number pattern	☐	☐	☐	Questions 3 to 4
draw the next pattern in a sequence.	☐	☐	☐	Questions 5 to 6

14 Perimeter and area of 2D shapes

Keywords: **perimeter, area**

1 Work out the **perimeter** of the following shapes drawn on a centimetre grid.
The first one has been done for you.

a

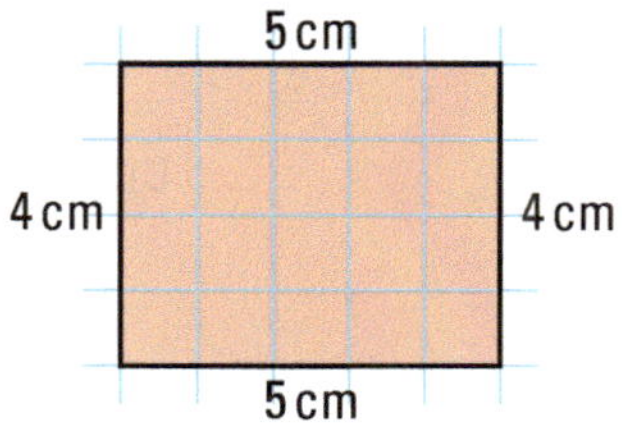

perimeter = 5 + 4 + 5 + 4 = 18 cm

b

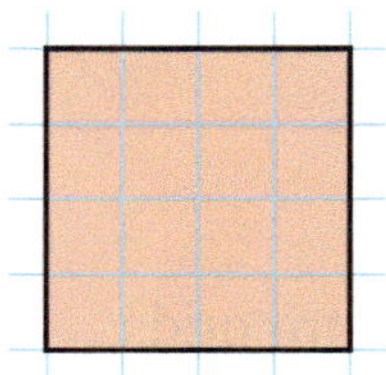

....

perimeter = ... cm

c

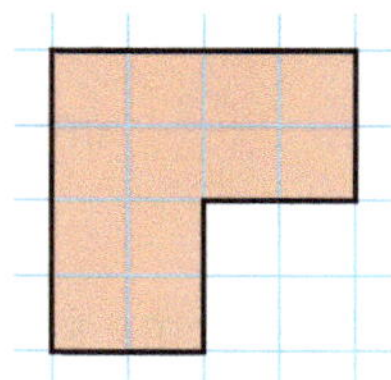

....

perimeter = ... cm

d

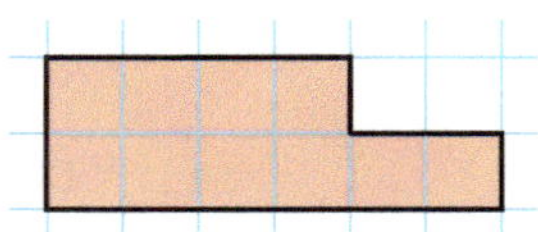

....

perimeter = ... cm

e

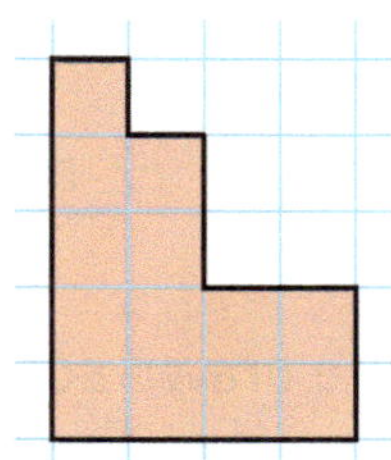

....

perimeter = ... cm

ResultsPlus Exam Tip

Remember: The perimeter is the total distance round the edge of the shape.

2 The diagram shows some shapes drawn on centimetre grids.

Find the **area** of each shape by counting the squares.
The first one has been done for you.

a

area = 12 cm^2

b

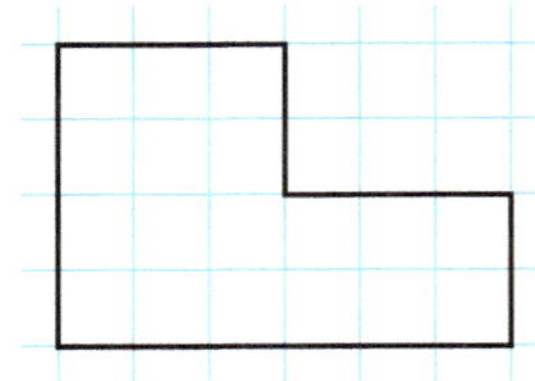

area = ... cm^2

c

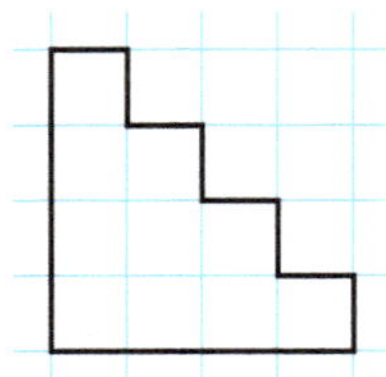

area = ... cm^2

3 The diagram shows some shapes drawn on centimetre grids.

Estimate the area of each shape by counting the squares.

a

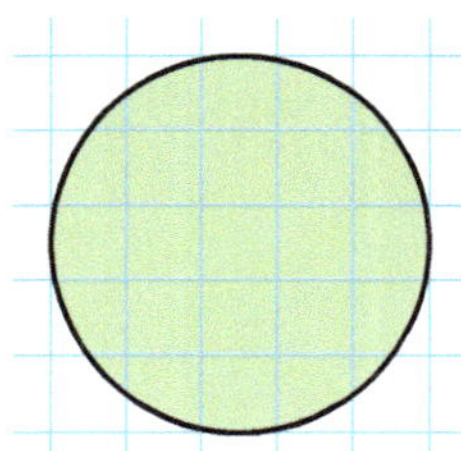

area = ... cm^2

b

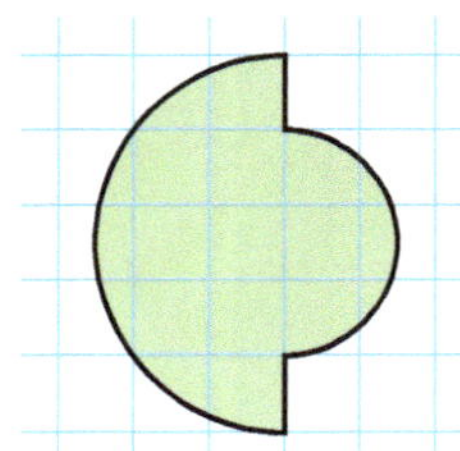

area = ... cm^2

4 These shapes are drawn accurately.
Find the perimeter of each shape.

a

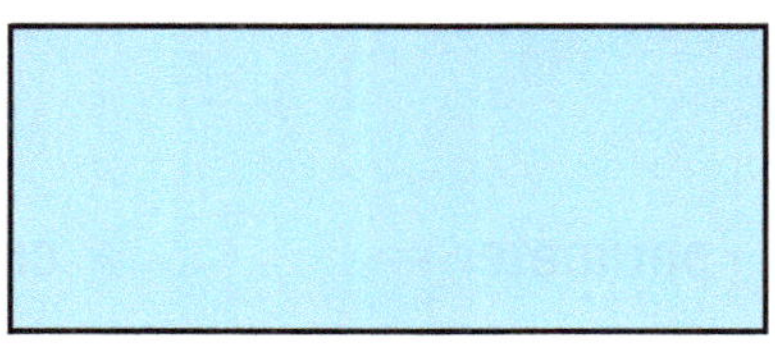

b

perimeter = ...

perimeter = ...

ResultsPlus
Exam Tip

Remember to write units with your answers.

5 Find the perimeter

a of a rectangle 3 cm wide and 8 cm long ....

b of a rectangle 11 cm wide and 15 cm long ....

c of a square patio 5 m by 5 m ....

6 Use the formula for the area of a rectangle to find the areas of the following shapes.
The first one has been done for you.

a

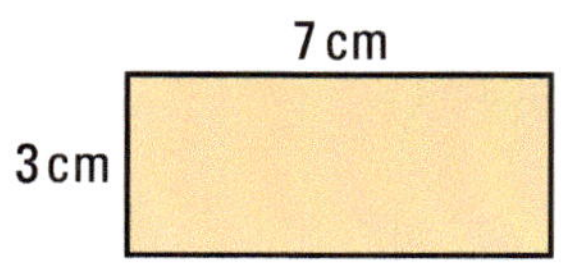

area $= 3 \times 7 = 21$ cm^2

b

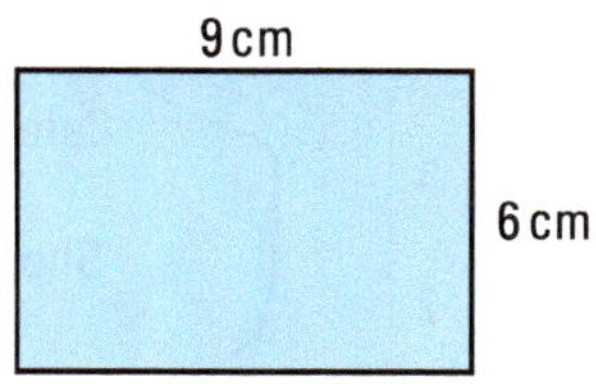

area = ... cm^2

c

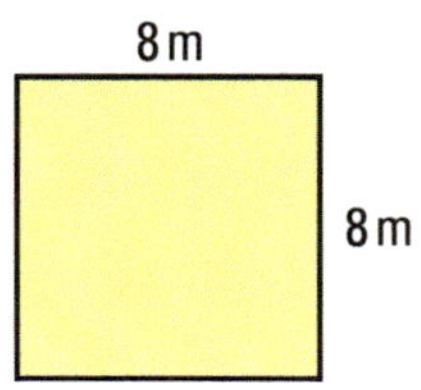

area = ... m^2

ResultsPlus Exam Tip

You can find the area of a rectangle by multiplying its length by its width.

Assess yourself

I can:				I can answer:	
find the perimeter of a simple shape	☐	☐	☐	Question 1	☐
find the area of a simple shape by counting squares	☐	☐	☐	Question 2	☐
estimate the area of an irregular shape by counting squares	☐	☐	☐	Question 3	☐
work out the perimeter of a rectangle	☐	☐	☐	Questions 4 to 5	☐
work out the area of a rectangle.	☐	☐	☐	Question 6	☐

15 Graphs 1

Keywords: **coordinates**

ResultsPlus Exam Tip

Remember to start at *O* and go along then up to find the coordinates.

1 Here is the map of a country park.

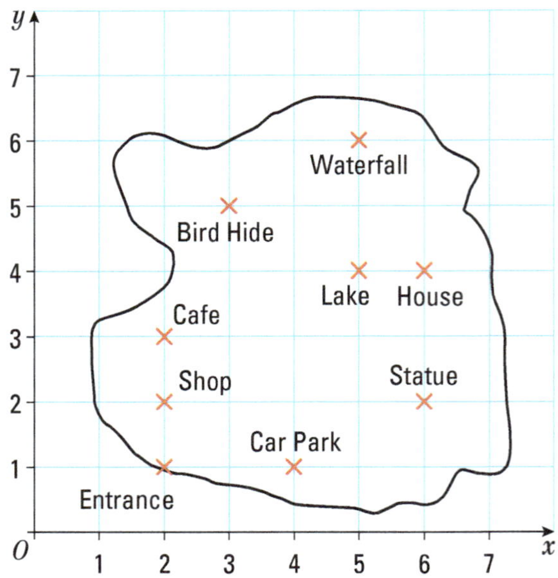

The **coordinates** of the Entrance are (2, 1).

a Write down the coordinates of these places on the map.

i Car Park (.......... , ...)

ii Bird Hide (.......... , ...)

iii House (.......... , ...)

iv Waterfall (.......... , ...)

b Write down what is at each point.

i (2, 3) ....

ii (6, 2) ....

iii (2, 2) ....

iv (5, 4) ....

2 Here is a coordinate grid.

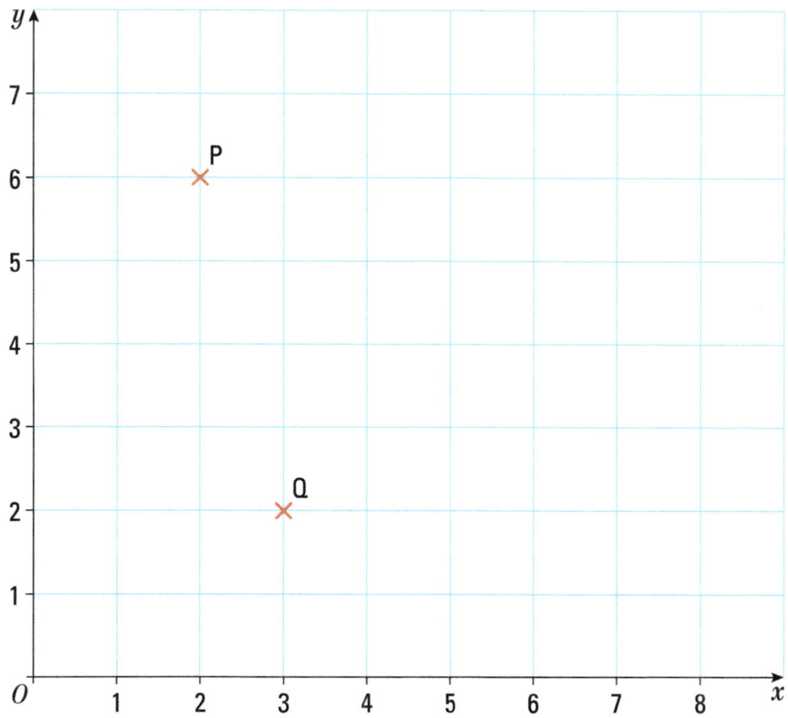

The points P and Q are shown on the grid.

On the grid, plot and label the points:

R (5, 4)   S (7, 2)   T (8, 6)

Join the points in the order PQRST with a ruler.

What letter of the alphabet is shown? ....

FS

3 The map shows a village.

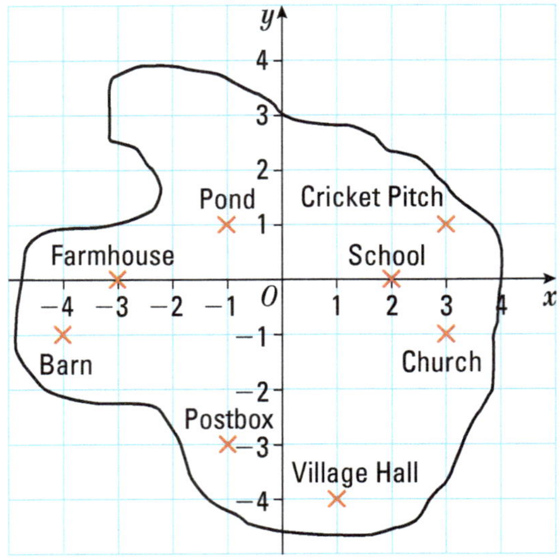

Fill in the missing coordinates and place names.

Place	Coordinates
School	(........, ...)
....	(3, 1)
Church	(3, ...)
Barn	(−4, ...)
....	(−3, 0)
Village Hall	(........, ...)
....	(−1, 1)
....	(........, −3)

Assess yourself

I can:				I can answer:
plot and use positive coordinates	☐	☐	☐	Questions 1 to 2
plot and use negative coordinates.	☐	☐	☐	Question 3

16 Averages and range

Keywords: **mode, median, mean, range**

1 Find the **mode** for each of the following lists of data.

a 6 11 8 5 9 12 8 7 8 9 11

....

b ham cheese chicken ham tuna tuna ham chicken chicken ham cheese

....

c 2.9 2.8 2.1 2.6 2.6 2.5 2.1 2.9 2.8 2.6 2.7 2.8

....

ResultsPlus Exam Tip

The mode is the data that is in a list most often.

2

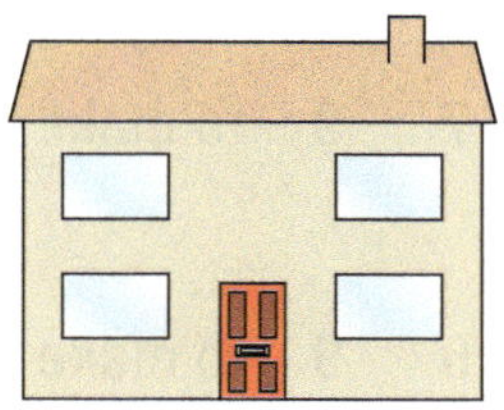

The list shows the number of letters a postman delivered to a house in one week.

3 4 2 3 2 1 3

Write down the mode. ....

3 Find the **median** for the following lists of data.

a 5 6 3 5 3 2 7 1 8

....

b 23 25 19 23 26 24 24

....

c 3.4 2.9 3.3 2.8 3.3 2.4 2.5 2.1 2.9

....

ResultsPlus Exam Tip

Arrange the numbers in order first then find the middle value.

AO2

ResultsPlus
Exam Tip

If there are two middle values the median is half way between them.

4 Find the median for the following lists of data:

a 2 3 4 3 2 6 7 6

....

b 12 14 12 13 14 15 16 17

....

c 25 15 30 60 80 20 50 40

....

AO2
AO3
FS

5 Here are some sets of spelling test marks.
Add a mark or marks to each set so that it has the mode or median shown.
The first has been done for you.

a 7 6 8 8 7 9 to make the mode 8, add 8 ....

b 9 10 8 7 6 9 to make the mode 7, add ....

c 7 6 8 8 7 9 to make the median 8, add ....

AO2
FS

ResultsPlus
Exam Tip

To find the mean add up the values then divide by the number of values in the list.

6 Find the **mean** of the following lists of data:

a 8 2 7 2 3 5 8

....

b 12 13 14 19 17 15

....

c 50 40 20 40 30 60 75

....

AO2 AO3

7 A group of children have a sponsored silence.
The list shows the amount of sponsor money each child got.

£5.00 £2.70 £3.00 £8.20 £3.21 £6.50 £4.00 £6.75 £9.60

What is the median amount of sponsor money?

....

....

AO2 FS

8 Find the **range** for each of the following lists of data.

a 3 5 2 7 1 8 12 3 4 2

....

b 21 24 17 12 13 17 21 23 24

....

ResultsPlus Exam Tip

The range = highest value − lowest value

FS

9 The table shows the mean monthly temperatures in London.

Month	Jan	Feb	Mar	Apr	May	Jun
Temperature °C	4	4	6	9	12	15

Month	Jul	Aug	Sep	Oct	Nov	Dec
Temperature °C	17	17	14	10	7	5

a Which are the coldest months? .... and ....

AO2 AO3

b What is the range of the temperature in London? ....

....

10 A group of students played 7 basketball matches.

The table shows the number of points three of the players scored in the 7 basketball matches.

	Match 1	Match 2	Match 3	Match 4	Match 5	Match 6	Match 7
Fliss	6	9	8	8	9	6	10
Ted	2	12	3	8	8	2	7
Jack	0	0	4	1	9	11	10

a Find the range of the scores for each player.

Fliss: .... Range ....

Ted: .... Range ....

Jack: .... Range ....

b Find the mean score for each player.

Fliss: .... Range ....

Ted: .... Range ....

Jack: .... Range ....

A02 A03

c The PE teacher is going to pick one of the three players to join the school team.

Which player should he pick? Give a reason for your answer.

Player: ....

Reason: ....

Assess yourself

I can:				I can answer:
find the mode for a data set	☐	☐	☐	Questions 1 to 2, 5 ☐
find the median	☐	☐	☐	Questions 3 to 5 ☐
calculate the mean	☐	☐	☐	Questions 6 to 7, 10 ☐
work out the range	☐	☐	☐	Questions 8 to 9 ☐
compare two sets of data using the range and an average.	☐	☐	☐	Question 10 ☐

17 Circles

Keywords: **diameter, radius**

1 Complete the following sentences.

a A circle has **radius** 5 cm.

The **diameter** of the circle is .... cm.

b A circle has radius 10.5 cm.

The diameter of the circle is .... cm.

c A circle has radius 7.4 cm.

The diameter of the circle is .... cm.

d A circle has radius 8.9 cm.

The diameter of the circle is .... cm.

e A circle has diameter 6 cm.

The radius of the circle is .... cm.

f A circle has diameter 9 cm.

The radius of the circle is .... cm.

g A circle has diameter 8.4 cm.

The radius of the circle is .... cm.

h A circle has diameter 12.8 cm.

The radius of the circle is .... cm.

ResultsPlus Exam Tip

The diameter of a circle is double the radius.

2 Some children drew around some leaves on centimetre-squared paper.

Estimate the area of each leaf by counting the squares.

ResultsPlus
Exam Tip

Remember that area is measured in square units.

a

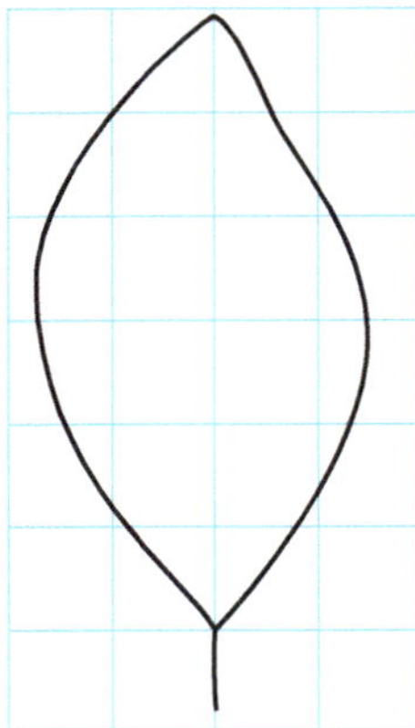

.... cm^2

b

.... cm^2

c

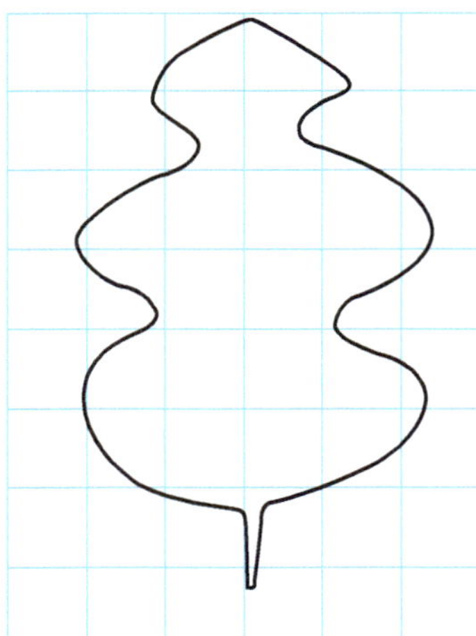

.... cm^2

d

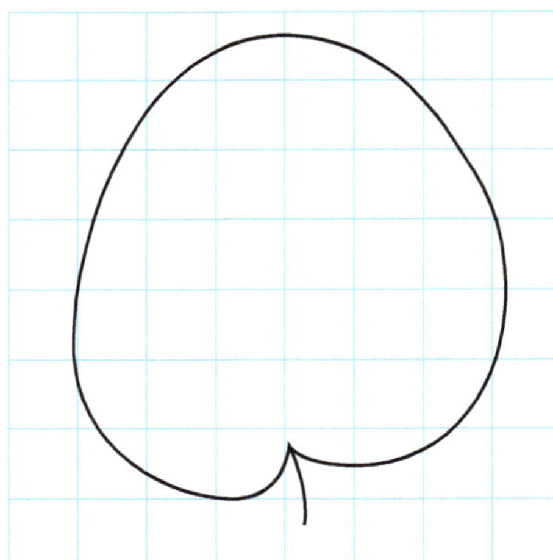

.... cm^2

3 These shapes have been drawn on centimetre-squared paper. Estimate the area of each shape.

a

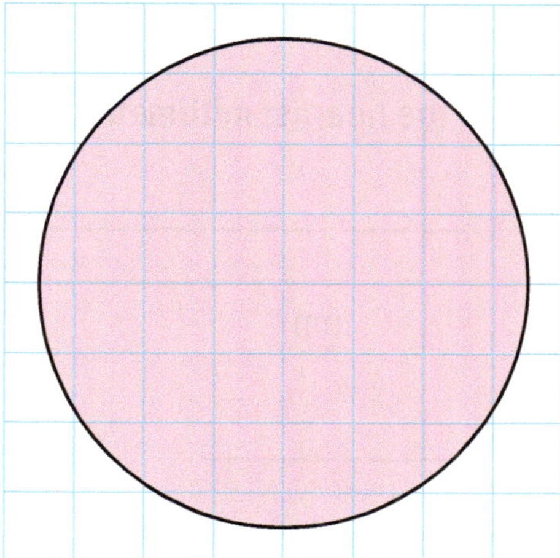

.... cm^2

b

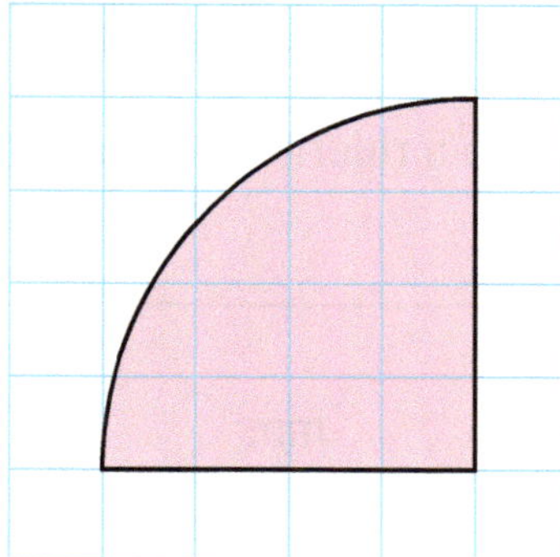

.... cm^2

c

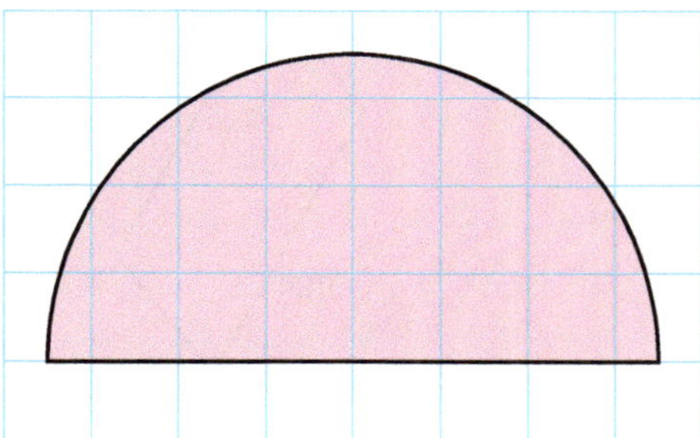

.... cm^2

d

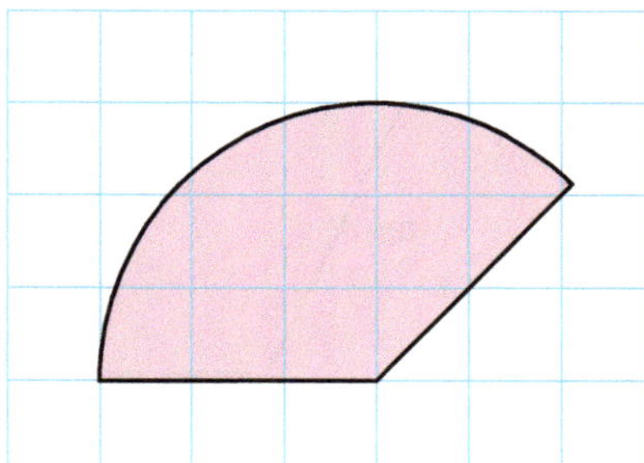

.... cm^2

Assess yourself

I can:				I can answer:	
understand the link between the radius and diameter of a circle	☐	☐	☐	Question 1	☐
estimate the area of irregular shapes by counting squares.	☐	☐	☐	Questions 2 to 3	☐

18 Constructions and loci

Keywords: **millimetre, length, degree, angle, 3-D shape**

1 Use a ruler to measure these lines to the nearest **millimetre**.

a ______________________________

.... mm

b ____

.... mm

c _________________________________

.... mm

d _____________________

.... mm

2 Measure the **lengths** of the sides of these shapes to the nearest millimetre.

a

.... mm

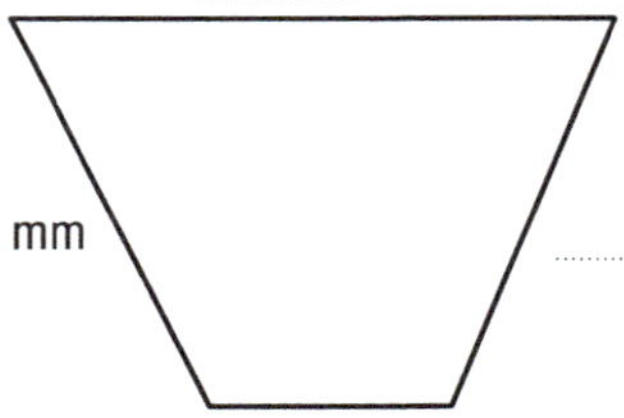

.... mm .... mm

.... mm

b

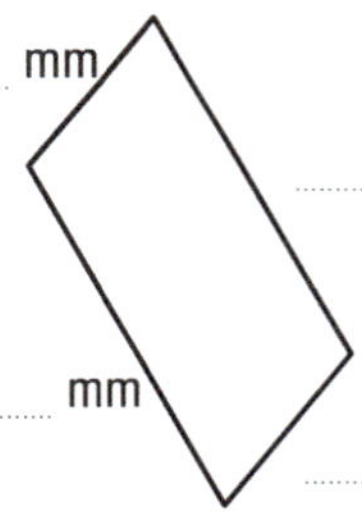

.... mm .... mm

.... mm .... mm

c

.... mm

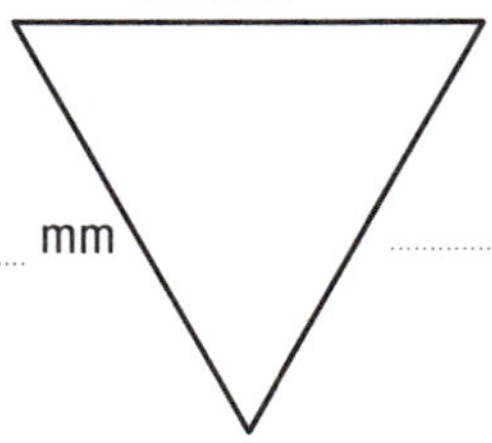

.... mm .... mm

d

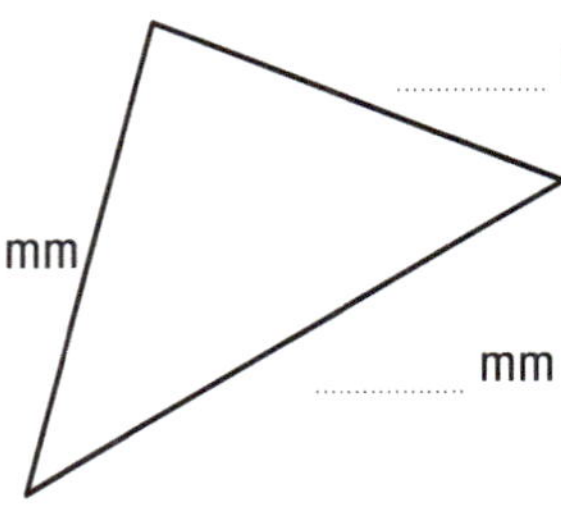

.... mm

.... mm

.... mm

3 Draw lines to match the net to the **3-D shape** it will make.

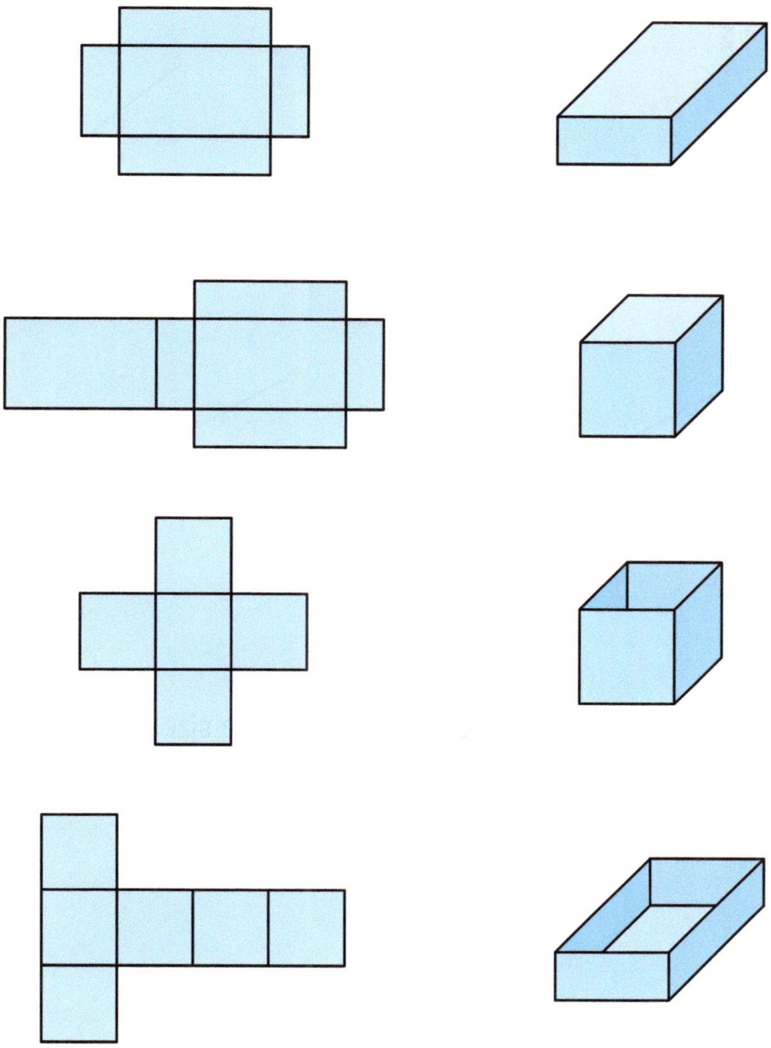

4 Match the pairs of lengths that are the same.
The first one has been done for you.

a 4 cm	40 cm
0.4 m	40 mm
400 cm	4 m
b 27 mm	0.27 m
27 cm	2.7 cm
2.7 m	270 cm

5 Use a protractor to measure these **angles** to the nearest **degree**.

a

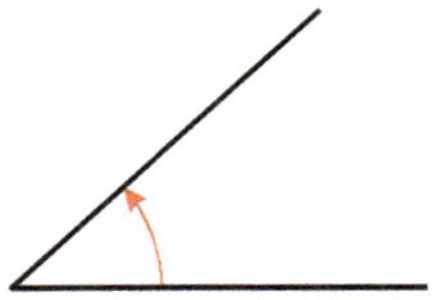

.... °

b

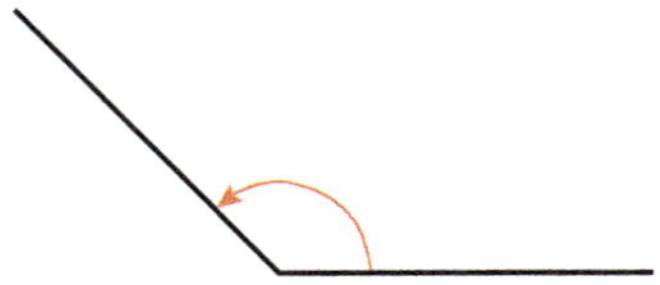

.... °

c

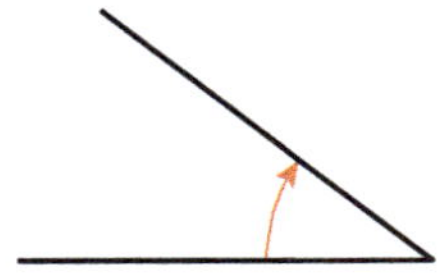

.... °

d

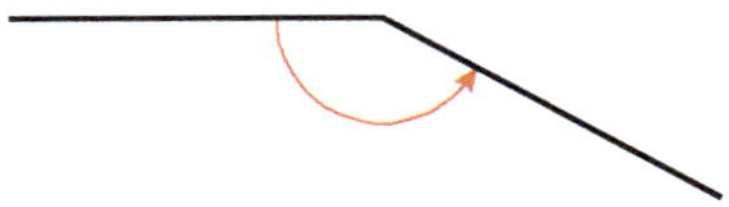

.... °

e

.... °

f

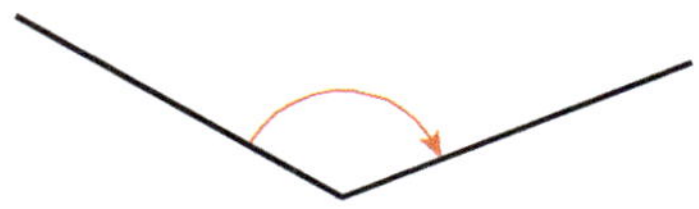

.... °

6 Use a ruler and protractor to draw angles of these sizes.

a 75°

b 142°

Assess yourself

I can:				I can answer:
measure lengths accurately	☐	☐	☐	Questions 1 to 2
recognise and draw the nets of simple 3-D shapes.	☐	☐	☐	Question 3
convert between millimetres and centimetres and between centimetres and metres	☐	☐	☐	Question 4
measure and draw angles to the nearest degree.	☐	☐	☐	Questions 5 to 6

19 Percentages

Keywords: **per cent or % means 'out of 100'**

1 90% of a football crowd is male.

What percentage is female? ....

2 52% of the days in a year are school days.

What percentage of days are **not** school days? ....

3 The table shows how pupils at Yatesbury School travel to school.

Bus	35%
Car	17%
Bicycle	6%
Walk	

What percentage of pupils walk to school? ....

4 Work out the percentages and match them with the answer.
One is done for you.

10% of £50	£40
20% of £50	£20
80% of £50	£28
50% of £40	£5
20% of £40	£8
70% of £40	£10

5 Luke has a part time job.
Each week he earns £40.
He spends 50% of this money on clothes.

How much is 50% of £40? £ ....

6 Susie buys a computer in a sale.
It normally costs £400.
There is 25% off in the sale.

How much cheaper is the computer in the sale? £ ....

FS

7 Julie bought a car for £6000.
The car loses 10% of its value in the first year.

What is 10% of £6000? £ ....

FS

8 There are 5 g of fat in 50 g of breakfast cereal.

What percentage is 5 g of 50 g? ....

FS

9 180 g of every 200 g of packaging can be recycled.

What percentage is 180 g of 200 g? ....

FS

10 The diagram shows the ages of people in the UK in 2008.

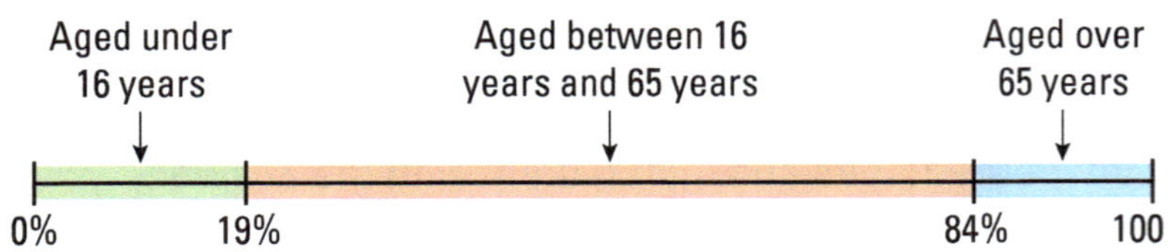

Use this information to complete the table.

Age	Percentage %
Under 16 years	
16–65 years	
Over 65 years	

Assess yourself

I can:				I can answer:
understand percentages	☐	☐	☐	Questions 1 to 3
work out percentages of quantities	☐	☐	☐	Question 4
solve problems using percentages.	☐	☐	☐	Questions 5 to 10

20 Three dimensional shapes

Keywords: **cone, cube, pyramid, sphere, cuboid, prism, cylinder**

1 Use a word from the box to name each 3-D shape.

cone	**cube**	**pyramid**	**sphere**

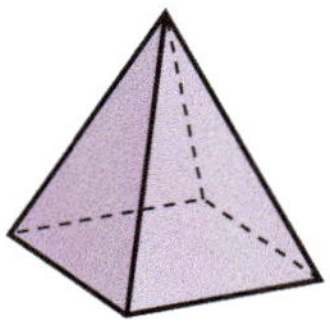

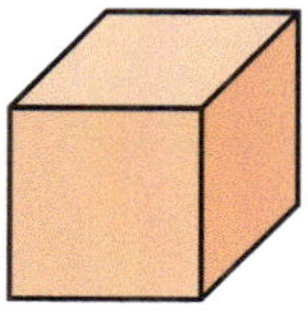

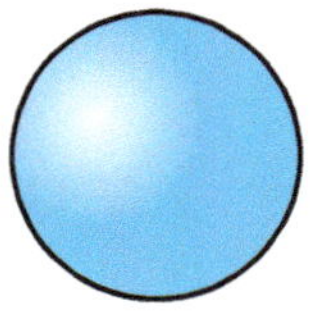

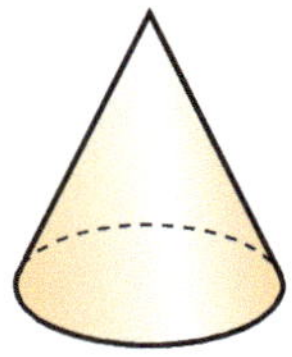

....

2 Draw a **cuboid** in the space below.

3 Draw a **cylinder** in the space below.

4 The diagrams below show some 3-D shapes made from centimetre cubes.
Find the volume of each shape.
Circle the one with a different volume.

a

.... cm^3

b

.... cm^3

c

.... cm^3

d

.... cm^3

5 The diagrams below show some 3-D shapes made from centimetre cubes. Find the volume of each prism.
Give the units with your answers.

a

....

b

....

c

....

6 Here is a triangular **prism**.

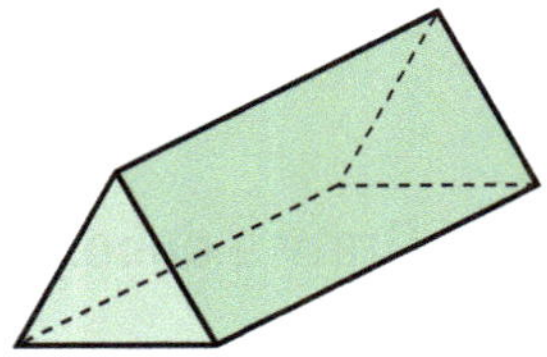

Complete the following.

Number of rectangular faces = ...

Number of triangular faces = ...

Total number of faces = ...

ResultsPlus Exam Tip

Remember to include the faces you can't see.

7 How many faces has a cube? .... faces

Assess yourself

I can:				I can answer:
name 3–D shapes	☐	☐	☐	Question 1
draw 3-D shapes	☐	☐	☐	Questions 2 to 3
find the volume of a solid by counting cubes	☐	☐	☐	Questions 4 to 5
find the number of faces of a 3-D shape.	☐	☐	☐	Questions 6 to 7

21 Equations and inequalities

Keywords: **output, input, algebra, equation, is less than, is greater than, is equal to**

1 Find the **output** from these **algebra** machines.

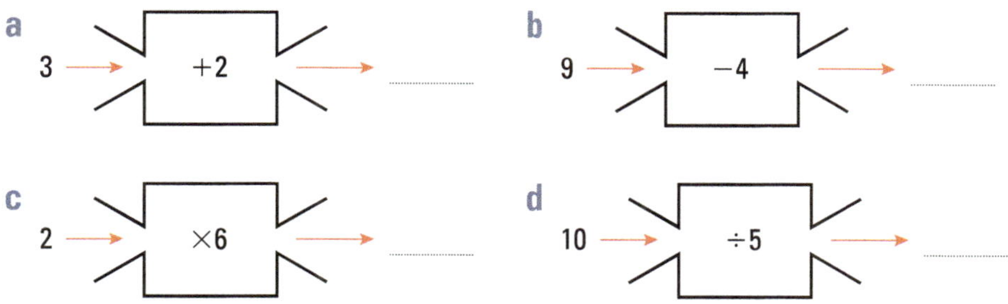

2 Find the **input** in these algebra machines.

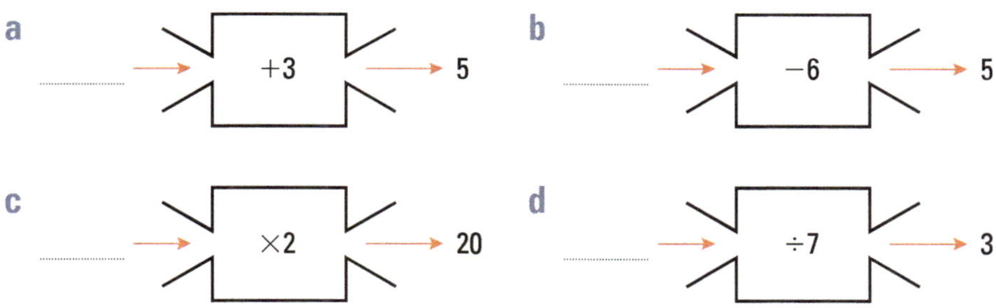

3 Katya thinks of a number.
She adds 5 and gets 12.

What number did Katya think of? ....

AO3

4 Tim thinks of a number.
He multiplies by 3 and gets 15.

What number did Tim think of? ....

AO3

5 Fill in the missing numbers.

a $12 - \ldots = 3$

b $7 + \ldots = 8$

c $3 \times \ldots = 33$

d $\ldots \div 6 = 6$

6 Choose the correct words from the list to complete each sentence.

is less than, is greater than, is equal to

a The number of apples .... the number of pears.

b The number of girls .... the number of boys.

c The number of cars .... the number of buses.

7 Here are the temperatures one day in four cities.

Berlin	London	Madrid	Paris
−4°C	1°C	7°C	−2°C

Circle the correct words in each sentence.

a The temperature in Paris is less than / is greater than the temperature in Madrid.

b The temperature in Berlin is less than / is greater than the temperature in Paris.

c The temperature in Berlin / London / Madrid / Paris is less than 0°C.

8 Jon thinks of a number.
He multiplies by 4, then adds 5. He gets 45.

What number did Jon think of? ....

9 Marie thinks of a number.
She subtracts 1 and then divides by 3. She gets 5.

What number did Marie think of? ....

10 Alfie has 23 CDs.
He buys x new CDs.
He now has 27 CDs.

Find the value of x. $x =$ ....

11 Anna has £y.
She shares it equally between 4 people.
Each person gets £2·50.

Find the value of y. $y =$ ....

A03

12 Solve each **equation**.

a $p + 2 = 6$

$p =$ ....

b $q - 5 = 8$

$q =$ ....

c $x + x = 12$

$x =$ ....

d $y + y + y = 6$

$y =$ ....

e $2a = 6$

$a =$ ....

f $5b = 20$

$b =$ ....

Assess yourself

I can:				I can answer:	
find inputs and outputs in algebra machines	☐	☐	☐	Questions 1 to 2	☐
solve word problems	☐	☐	☐	Questions 3 to 4, 8 to 9	☐
use statements to compare the size of numbers	☐	☐	☐	Questions 6 to 7	☐
solve equations.	☐	☐	☐	Questions 10 to 12	☐

22 Graphs 2

Keywords: **coordinates**

1 Fill in the missing **coordinates**.

A (........ , ...)

B (........ , ...)

C (........ , ...)

D (3, 4)

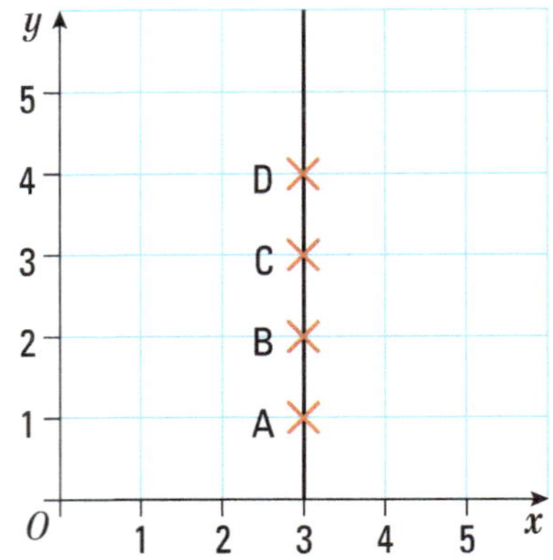

2 Here are three points.

P (0, 2)   **Q** (2, 2)   **R** (5, 2)

a Plot the points on the grid

b Join the points with a ruler to make a straight line.

c Write down the coordinates of another point on this line.

(........ , ...)

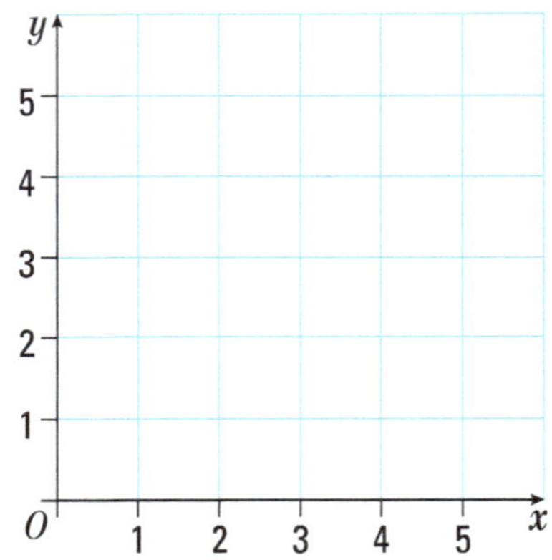

3 Fill in the missing values so that the points all lie on the straight line shown.

(0, ...)

(2, ...)

(........ , 3)

(−1, ...)

(........ , −2)

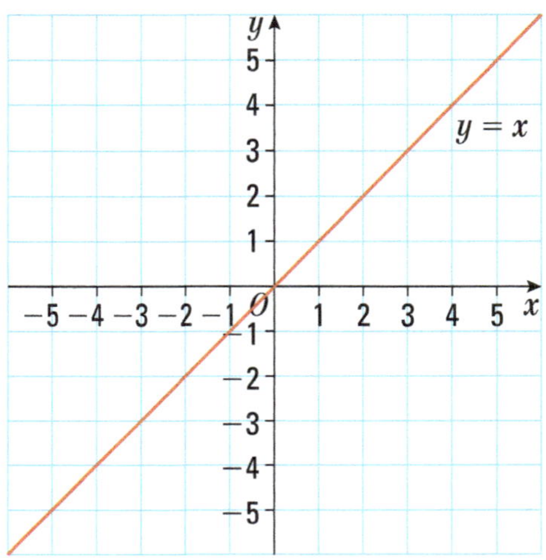

4 **a** On the grid, plot T (1, 2)
U (3, 4)
V (−2, −1).

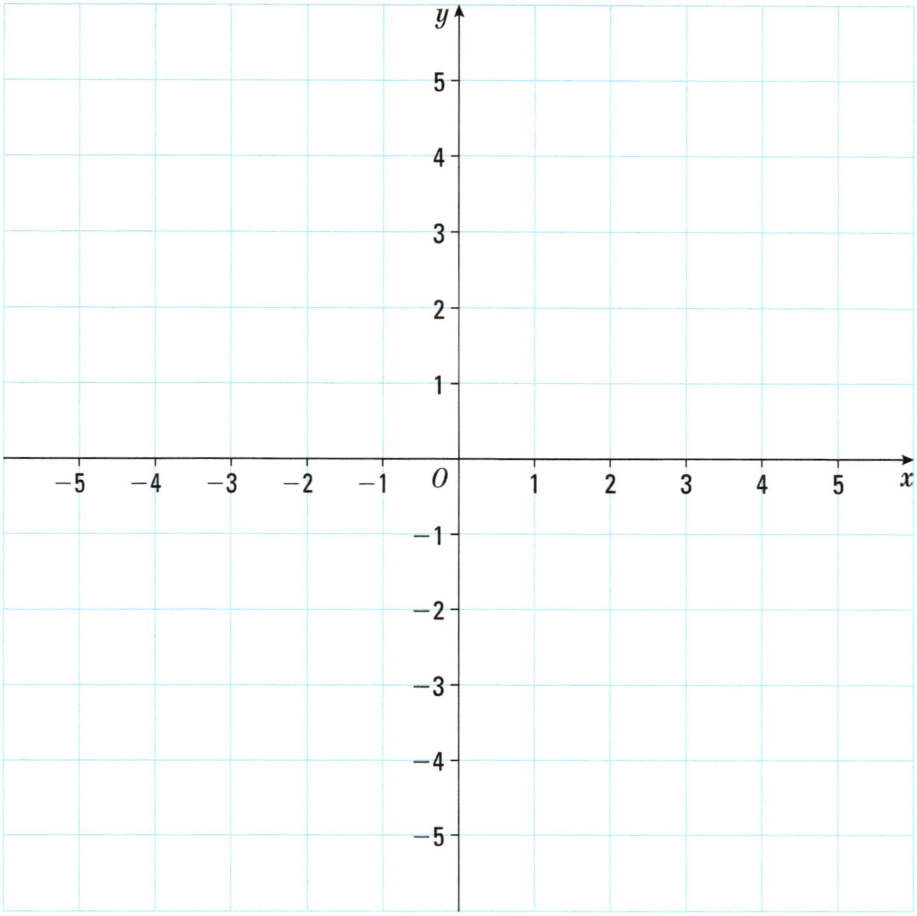

b Join the points with a ruler to make a straight line.

c Label the line $y = x + 1$.

Assess yourself

I can:				I can answer:	
plot points on a grid	☐	☐	☐	Questions 1 to 4	☐
write down the coordinates of points.	☐	☐	☐	Questions 1 to 4	☐

23 Transformations

Keywords: **line of symmetry, reflection, mirror line, order of rotation, scale factor, enlargement**

1 Draw in the line of reflection on each pair of shapes.

a

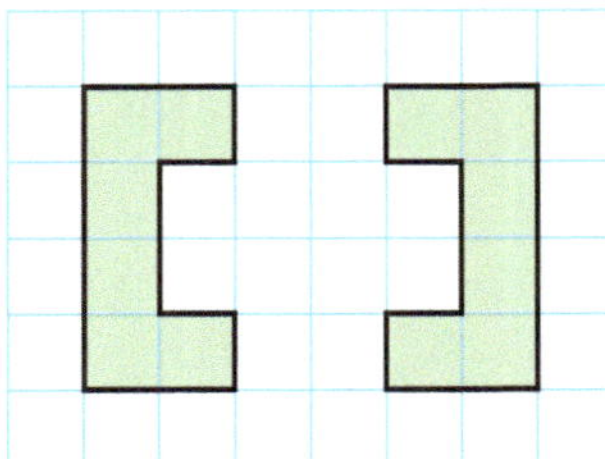

b

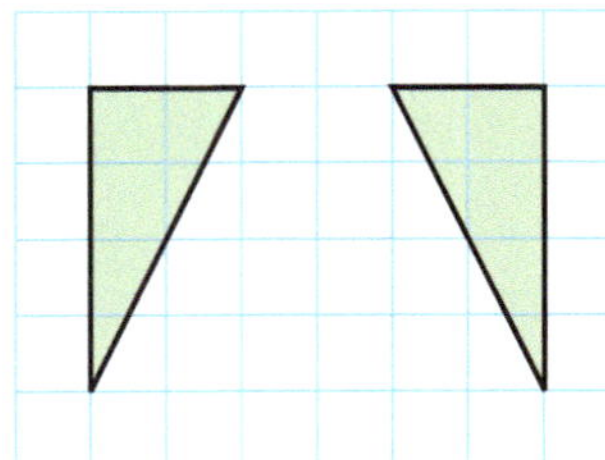

c

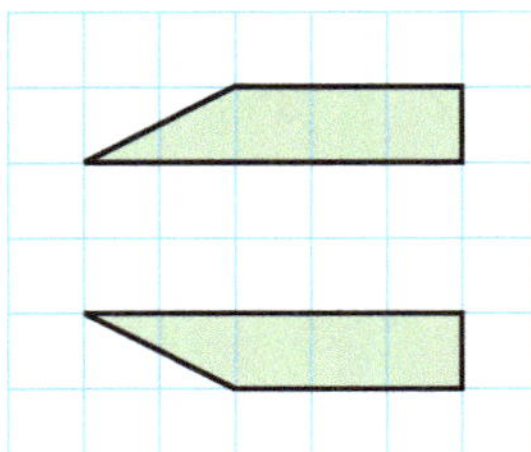

d

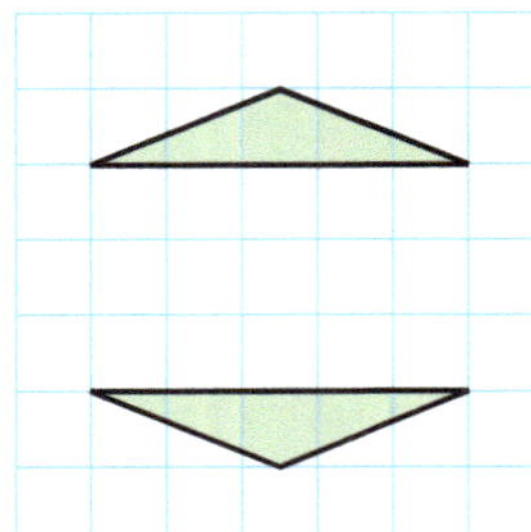

ResultsPlus Exam Tip

Remember to use a ruler and pencil for drawing.

2 In the diagram the dotted lines are **lines of symmetry**.

Draw the **reflection** of each shape in its **mirror line**.

a

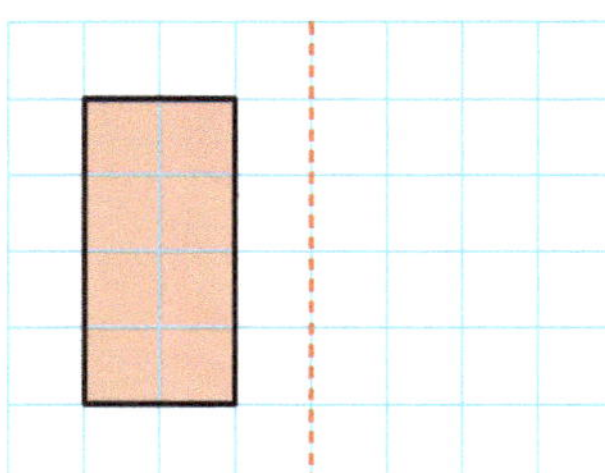

b

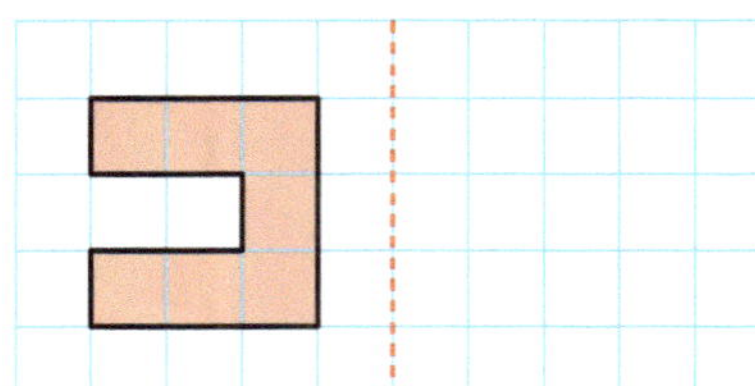

c

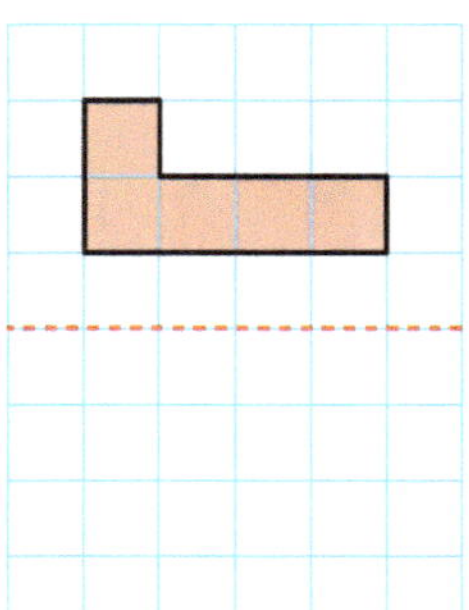

d

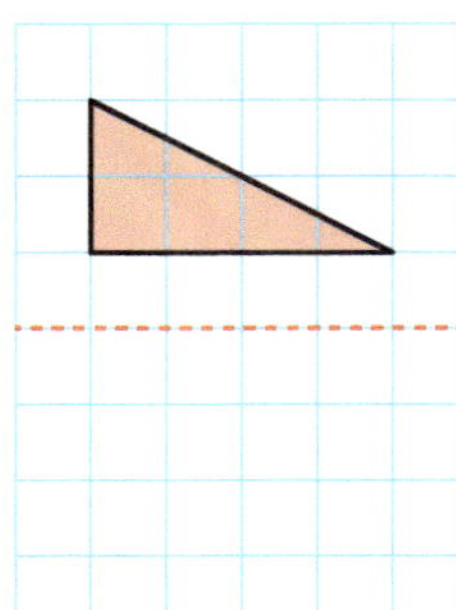

3 The pictures show some letters of the alphabet.

Draw the lines of symmetry on the letters.

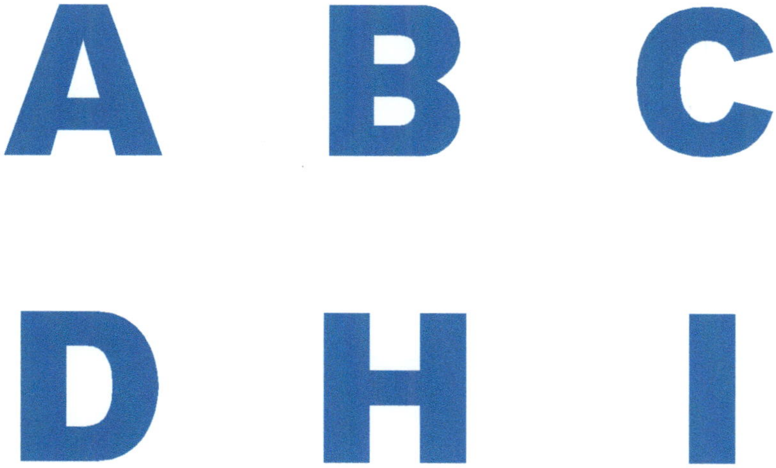

4 These letters are from different alphabets.

Write down the **order of rotation** of each letter.

a .... b .... c .... d .... e ....

f .... g .... h .... i .... j ....

5 Write down the **scale factor** of the **enlargement** from A to B for each pair of shapes.

ResultsPlus
Exam Tip

The **scale factor** is the number by which lengths have been multiplied.

a

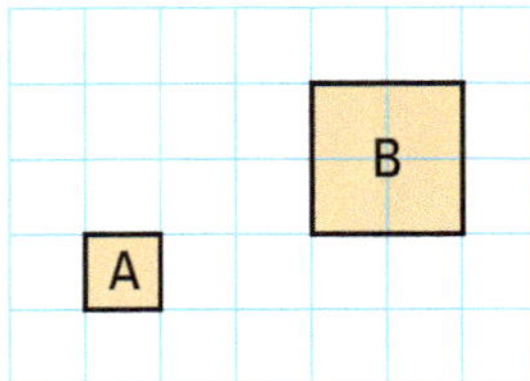

b

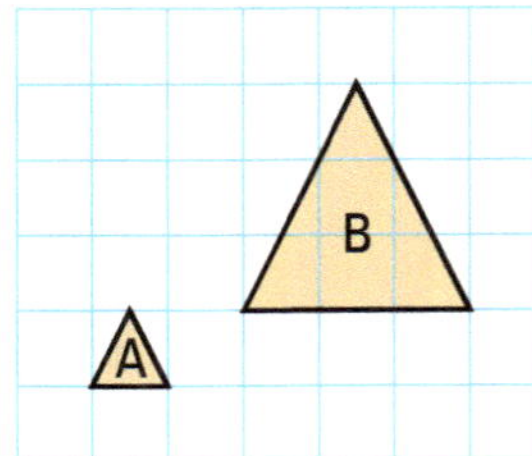

c

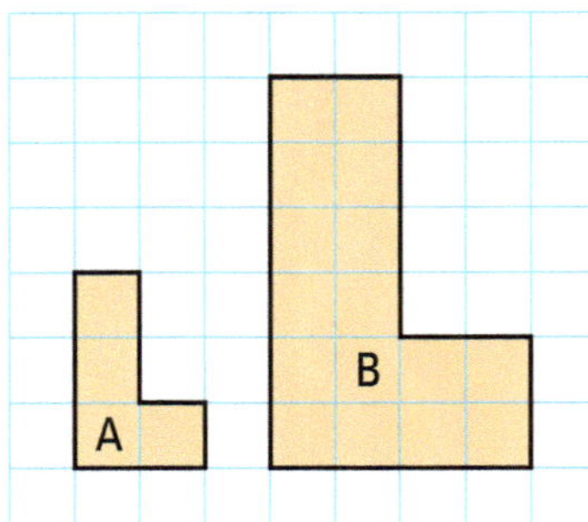

d

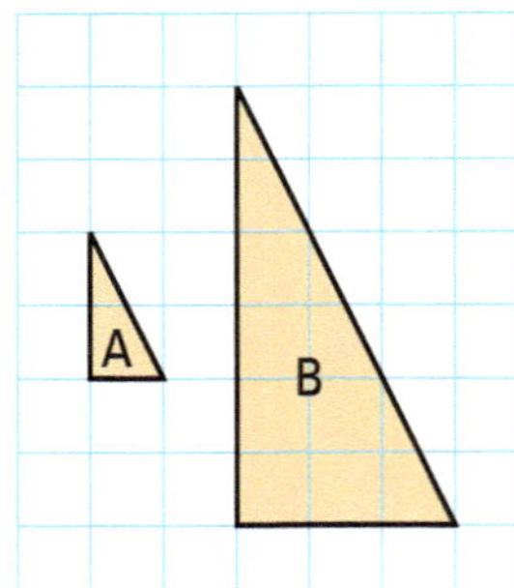

Assess yourself

I can:				I can answer:
draw the line of reflection for two shapes	☐	☐	☐	Question 1
draw the reflection of a shape in a mirror line	☐	☐	☐	Question 2
draw lines of symmetry on a shape	☐	☐	☐	Question 3
give the order of rotation of a shape	☐	☐	☐	Question 4
give the scale factor of an enlargement.	☐	☐	☐	Question 5

24 Ratio and proportion

Keywords: **simplify, equivalent fractions, ratio**

1 There are twice as many blue tiles as white tiles on a kitchen floor.

a In Daniel's kitchen there are 10 white tiles.

How many blue tiles are there? .... blue tiles

b In Hajra's kitchen there are 40 blue tiles.

How many white tiles are there? .... white tiles

FS A03

2 There are some cars and some motorbikes in a car park.
There are three times the number of cars as the number of motorbikes.

How many cars and motorbikes are there?
Tick (✓) the correct answer.

3 cars 1 motorbike	2 cars 6 motorbikes	10 cars 30 motorbikes	25 cars 25 motorbikes
....	....	....	....

3 There are some chocolates in a box.
There are 4 milk chocolates for every white chocolate.

There are 5 white chocolates.

How many milk chocolates are there? .... milk chocolates

«

4 **Simplify** each fraction.
The first one is done for you.

a $\frac{5}{10} = \frac{1}{2}$

b $\frac{3}{9} =$ ....

c $\frac{2}{12} =$ ....

d $\frac{10}{50} =$ ....

e $\frac{6}{8} =$ ....

f $\frac{15}{25} =$ ....

«««

5 $\frac{1}{2}, \frac{2}{4}, \frac{3}{6}$ and $\frac{4}{8}$ all have the same value.
They are **equivalent fractions**.

Write down 3 more fractions equivalent to $\frac{1}{2}$ ...., ..., ...

Write down 3 fractions equivalent to $\frac{1}{8}$ ...., ..., ...

Write down 3 fractions equivalent to $\frac{2}{3}$ ...., ..., ...

Assess yourself

I can:				I can answer:
use proportions	☐	☐	☐	Questions 1 to 3
find equivalent fractions.	☐	☐	☐	Questions 4 to 5

25 Line diagrams and scatter graphs

Keywords: **graph, bar chart**

FS

1 Fernando is going on holiday to Singapore.
He gets 2 Singapore dollars for £1.

a How many Singapore dollars does he get for £2? ....

b How many Singapore dollars does he get for £10? ....

c Complete the table:

British pounds	1	2	3	4	5	6	7	8	9	10
Singapore dollars	2					12				

d Plot the points on the graph. Two of the points have been plotted for you.

e Join the points on the graph with a straight line.

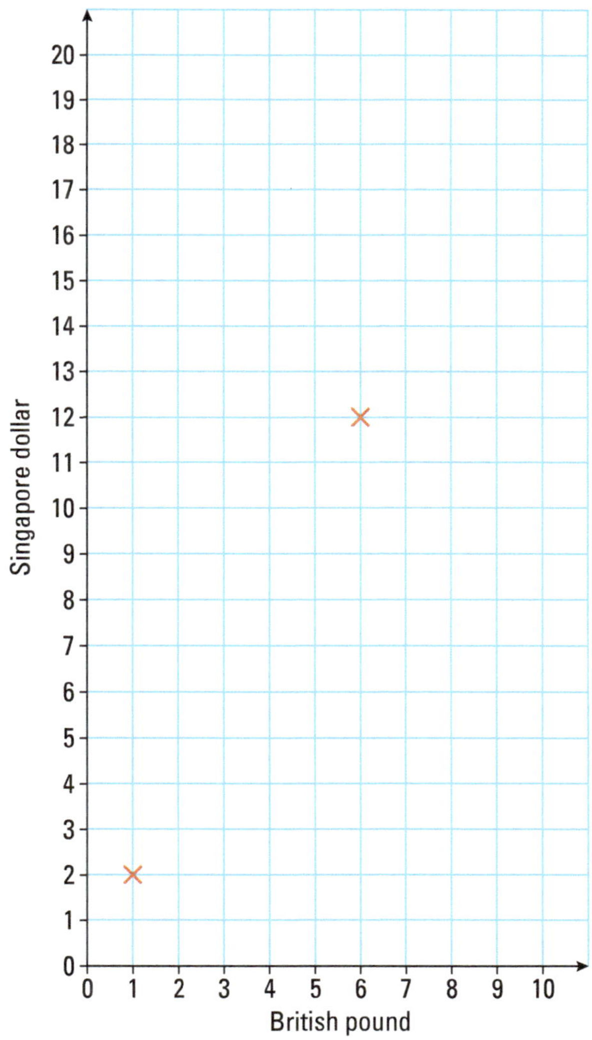

f Fernando changes £7.50 into Singapore dollars.

Use your graph to work out the number of Singapore dollars he gets.

2 John needs 20p coins for a pinball machine. He only has pound coins.

a How many 20p coins will he get for £2? ....

b Complete the table:

Number of £1 coins	1	2	3	4	5	6	7	8	9	10
Number of 20p coins					25			40		

c Plot the points on the **graph**.

Two of the points have been plotted for you.

d Join the points on the graph.

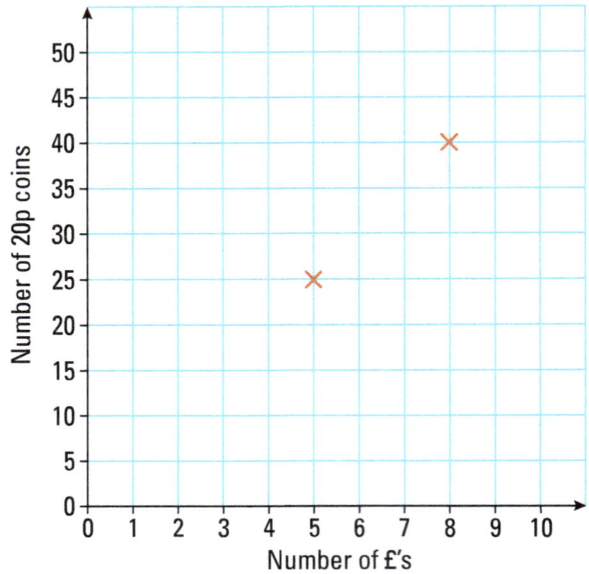

ResultsPlus
Exam Tip

Remember to use a sharp pencil to plot your points and use a ruler to draw a straight line.

e John has £9.

Use your graph or table to work out the number of 20p coins he will get for £9.

....

Assess yourself

I can:				I can answer:	
draw and interpret a conversion graph	☐	☐	☐	Questions 1 and 2	☐
plot points from a table	☐	☐	☐	Questions 1 and 2	☐
complete a table of values.	☐	☐	☐	Questions 1 and 2	☐

26 Probability

Keywords: **event, probability, probability scale, fair, outcome, random**

1 Match each **event** to the correct probability.
The first one has been done for you.

Events	Probabilities
You will present the TV news in one hour	Unlikely
You will see a dog on the way home	Likely
You flip a coin and get a head	Certain
The sun will rise tomorrow	Impossible
You will be late to school tomorrow	Even chance

2 Choose a **probability** word from the box to complete each of the following sentences.

unlikely	likely	certain	impossible	even chance

a I am .... to walk home from school today.

b It is .... that it will rain this winter.

c I am .... to see my friends this weekend.

d It is .... that the sky will be green tomorrow.

«

3 Draw arrows to put each event in the correct place on the **probability scale**. One of them has been done for you.

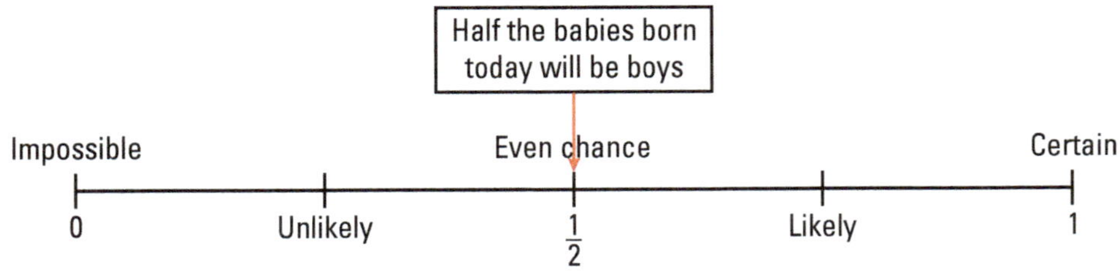

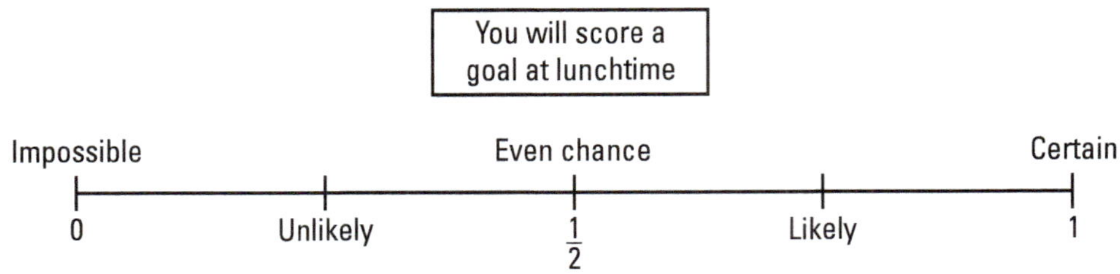

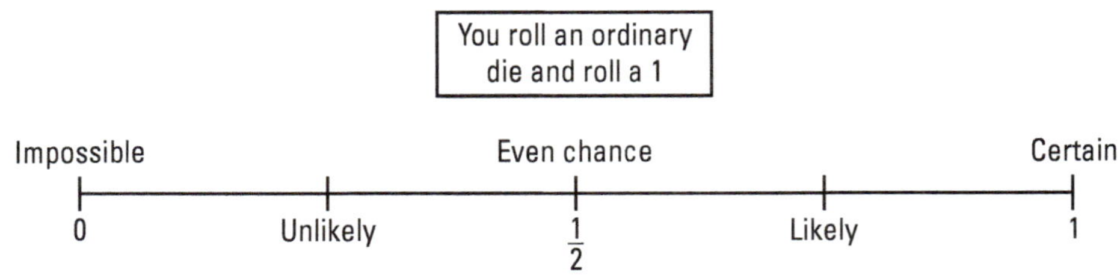

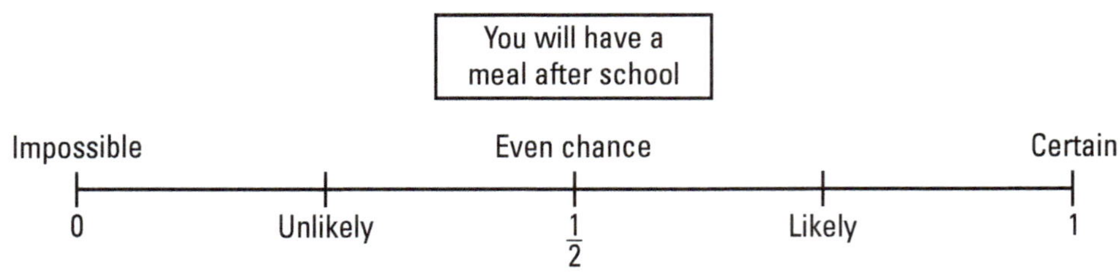

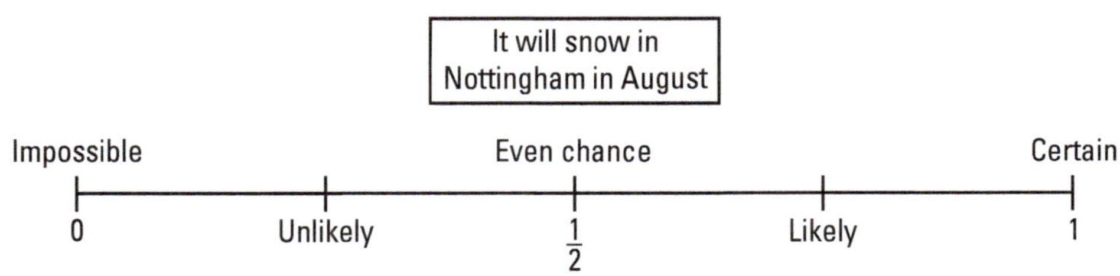

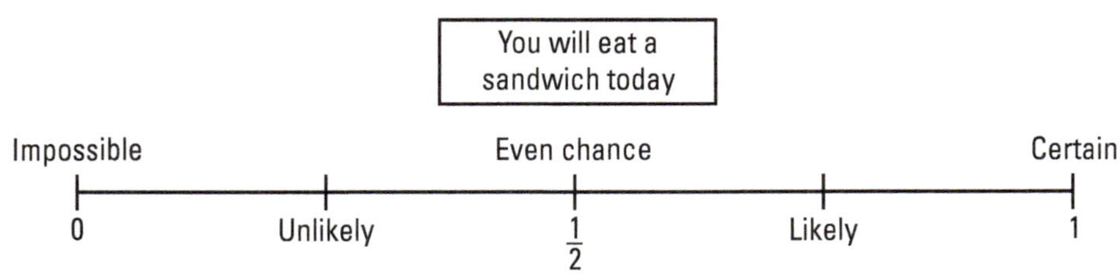

4 Write down all the possible outcomes for each of the following events: A02

a rolling an ordinary die ______________________________

b a football match ______________________________

c spinning a coin ______________________________

5 Complete the spinners so that they will have the correct outcomes. A02 A03

a Four equally likely outcomes:
red, yellow, blue and green.

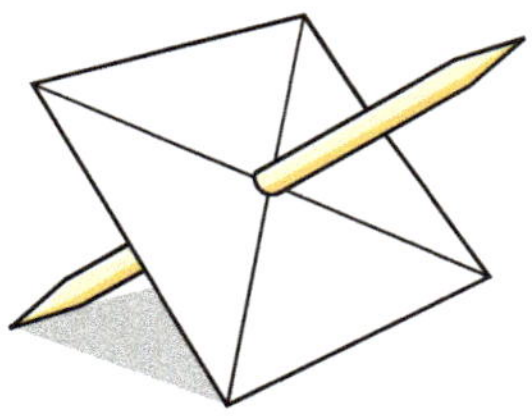

b Eight equally likely outcomes:
1, 2, 3, 4, 5, 6, 7, 8.

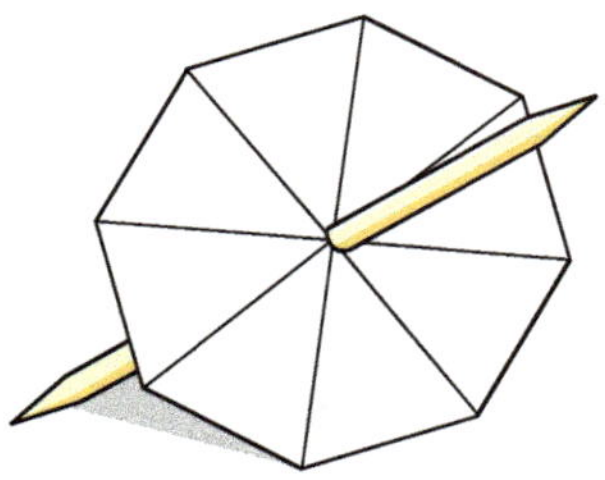

Assess yourself

I can:				I can answer:	
use the vocabulary of probability	☐	☐	☐	Questions 1 to 3	☐
use the probability scale	☐	☐	☐	Questions 1 to 3	☐
list all the outcomes of an event in a logical way.	☐	☐	☐	Questions 4 to 5	☐

27 Pythagoras' Theorem

Keywords: **triangle, square, square root, area**

«

1 Here are some triangles.

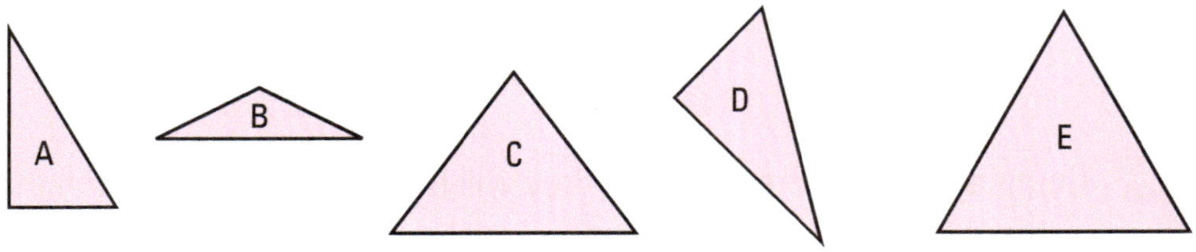

Circle the letter to complete each statement correctly.

a The equilateral **triangle** is A B C D E

b The isosceles triangles are A B C D E

c The right-angled triangles are A B C D E

A02

2 Durgesh makes some square patterns using coloured tiles.

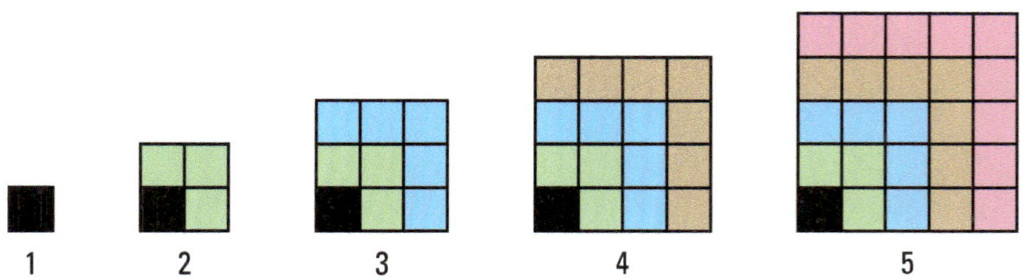

Fill in the table to show how many tiles of each colour there are in each pattern. The first two rows are done for you.

Pattern number	Number of black tiles	Number of green tiles	Number of blue tiles	Number of brown tiles	Number of pink tiles	Total number of tiles
1	1	0	0	0	0	1
2	1	3	0	0	0	4
3						
4						
5						

3 Find the **area** of these **squares**.

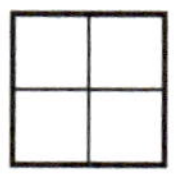

Area = ... cm^2

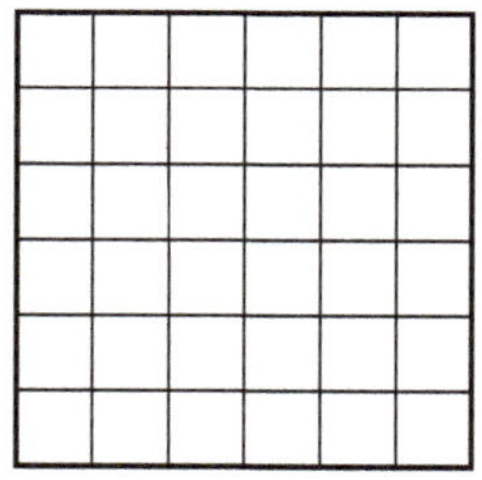

Area = ... cm^2

Key

☐ represents 1 cm^2

4 Work out the area of these squares.

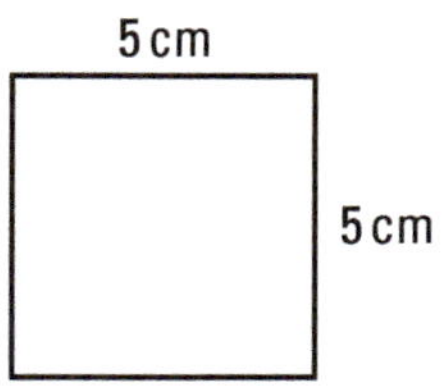

Area = ... cm^2

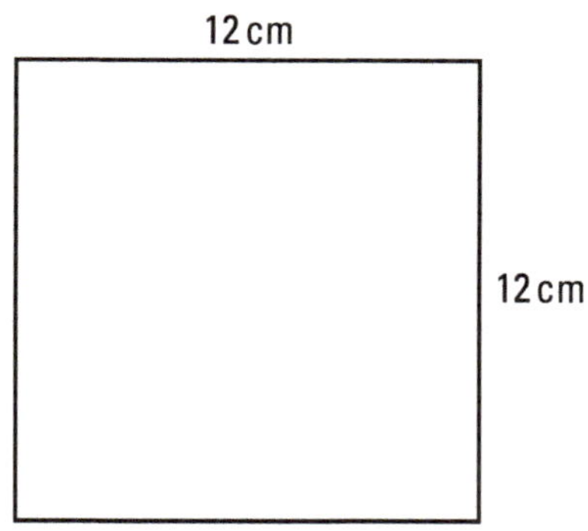

Area = ... cm^2

5 Circle the numbers in the cloud that are square numbers.

6 Work out the value of these square numbers.

a $10^2 = 10 \times 10 =$ ....

b $8^2 =$ ....

c $12^2 =$ ....

7 Work out the value of these **square roots**.

a $\sqrt{16}$ = ... **b** $\sqrt{81}$ = ... **c** $\sqrt{121}$ = ...

8 Work out the value of:

a 4.5^2 = ... **b** $\sqrt{56.25}$ = ... **c** $3^2 + 9^2$ = ...

A02

9 Here is a right-angled triangle.
A square is drawn on each side of the triangle.

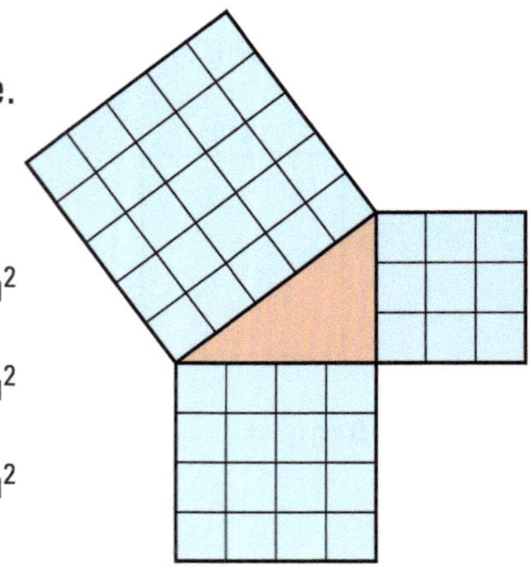

Fill in the missing answers below:

Area of the 3 cm by 3 cm square = ... cm^2

Area of the 4 cm by 4 cm square = ... cm^2

Area of the 5 cm by 5 cm square = ... cm^2

What do you notice about your answers?

....

....

Assess yourself

I can:				I can answer:
name special triangles	☐	☐	☐	Question 1
find the area of a square	☐	☐	☐	Questions 2 to 4
work out squares and square roots	☐	☐	☐	Questions 5 to 8
quote Pythagoras' Theorem.	☐	☐	☐	Question 9

28 Formulae

Keywords: **expression, formula**

1 Apples cost 15p each.

Use the **formula**

cost = number of apples × 15

to work out the cost of 3 apples ....

A02

2 Emile works for 12 hours.

He is paid an hourly rate of £7 an hour.

Use the formula

pay = hourly rate × hours worked

to work out Emile's pay. ....

A02

3 Here is a formula to work out the perimeter of a square.

Perimeter = 4 × side length

Use the formula to work out the perimeter of the following squares.

a side length 4 cm ....

b side length 6 cm ....

c side length 5 m ....

d side length 8 m ....

A02

4 Write an **expression** for the following sentences.
The first one is done for you.

a Multiply m by 3 and add 4 $3m + 4$

b Add 7 to p ....

c Multiply n by 2 ....

d Multiply q by 5 and take away 1 ....

e Subtract 6 from d ....

f Multiply c by 5 and subtract 2 ....

A02

5 The diagram shows the radius and the diameter of a circle.

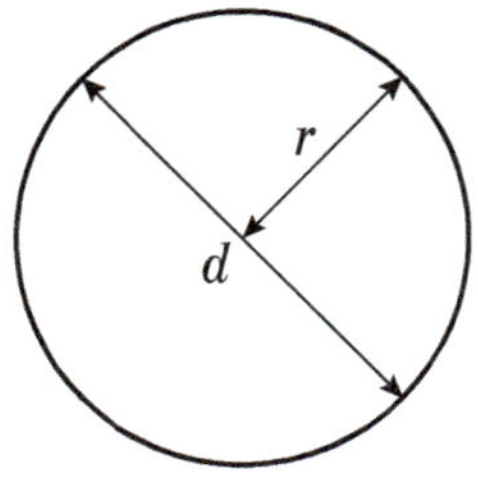

Circle the correct formula below to link the radius and diameter of a circle.

$d = r + 2$ $\quad$ $d = r \div 2$ $\quad$ $d = 2r$ $\quad$ $d = r - 2$ $\quad$ $r = 2d$

6 Circle the correct sentence for this expression.

$6 - d$

Subtract 6 from d $\quad$ Subtract d from 6

7 Circle the correct sentence for this expression.

$p + 6$

Add 6 to p $\quad$ Multiply p by 6

8 $h = 5$

Use the formula $w = 6h$ to work out w. $\quad$ $w =$ ....

9 $t = 8$

$s = 20 + t$

Work out the value of s. $\quad$ $s =$ ....

AO3

10 $x = 4$

$y = x + 5$

Work out the value of y. $y =$ ....

11 $y = 12$

$y = x + 3$

Work out the value of x. $x =$ ....

12 $x = 5$

$y = x + 10$

Work out the value of y. $y =$ ....

13 $y = 25$

$y = x + 10$

Work out the value of x. $x =$ ....

Assess yourself

I can:	Red	Amber	Green	I can answer:	
use formulae to work out values	☐	☐	☐	Questions 1 to 3 and 6 to 13	☐
write down expressions	☐	☐	☐	Question 4	☐
write down formulae.	☐	☐	☐	Question 5	☐

Published by Pearson Education Limited, a company incorporated in England and Wales, having its registered office at Edinburgh Gate, Harlow, Essex, CM20 2JE. Registered company number: 872828

Edexcel is a registered trademark of Edexcel Limited

First published 2010

13
10 9 8 7 6 5 4 3

British Library Cataloguing in Publication Data
A catalogue record for this book is available from the British Library.

ISBN 978 1 84690675 6

Typeset by Tech-Set Ltd, Gateshead
Printed in Great Britain by CPI Group (UK) Ltd, Croydon, CR0 4YY